DEFRIENDING FACEBOOK

How I deactivated my account
& re-activated my life

A MEMOIR BY RACHEL RUFF

Samantha Martin, *Copy editor*
John Dedakis, *Line editor*
Matthew Legrice, *Web Designer, Cover Artist*
Danielle Vala, *Layout Designer*
Jessica Saba, *Agent*
Karl Osterbuhr, *Photography*
Ashley Salt, *Hair*
Eve boutique, *Wardrobe*

**Printed in the United States of America
Second Printing, 2014**

defriendingfacebook.com

FOR MY GRAMA SAM
Rachel Ruff: is missing you.

AUTHOR'S NOTE

This is my truth as I remember it. I have open heartedly uncovered my own social media secrets within this book to clearly detail how I came to extricate myself from an online obsession with Facebook. Details on some of the persons with whom I was in Facebook contact and related events were changed in order to protect their identities.—RR

TABLE OF CONTENTS

INTRODUCTION

Life in the fast lane as a CNN documentary producer and then as a vice president of a world-renowned PR agency came to a screeching halt when I parked myself on Facebook.

I joined Facebook in 2006 and my friend list grew from 1 to 1,500 friends in just over two years. Facebook was a way for me to medicate my real life boredom pains. I began spending my days looking at what my thousand-plus friends were busy doing in life, or at least what I thought they were doing, and I couldn't help compare myself to them.

During the four years I belonged to Facebook, I would get a high when someone would post a hello to my wall. Devising witty yet completely bogus status updates to conceal the true boredom and loneliness I was feeling was my ecstasy. A strong hit of the "thumbs up" button from friends to show their "like" beneath my wall photos and I would become digitally drunk. Had there been a Facebook-alyzer hooked up to the computer monitor, I probably would have blown an 8.0.

Where was an operator's manual to show me how to properly engage in Facebook and to inform me to steer clear of the urge to sensationalize my life? Facebook for Dummies only addressed the technical functionalities of the site. I needed a "Facebook for Addicts and Fakers" to help me solve the enigma of who I was becoming online versus who I truly was offline. One post after another, year after year, the web of self-deceit, gossip, frenemies, and false cheer I spun on my Facebook wall became too intricate for me to untangle. I had let my reality become obscured with the quest for Facebook glory. I had become addicted to Facebook, like a bad romance. I'd gotten so caught up in growing my own profile that I wasn't honest with myself about how hard it was to live up to my own hype. I stopped loving myself. I was a Fakebooker and a posting poser. And then I hit rock bottom.

This book is my story of how Facebook came to dominate my life, and how I finally said enough is enough. Unfortunately, I couldn't easily turn my back on my social media obsession. I needed a methodical way to unleash myself from my Facebook obsession, so I devised a five-stage plan, similar to one used by an addict of alcohol or substance abuse. The "De-friending Facebook" guidelines I created and taped to the wall over my computer saved my life, both literally and figuratively. These guidelines enabled me to break up with "Mr. Facebook."

My story is one that is becoming all too familiar for many social media users. How do we navigate our online world without letting it encroach on our real world? How do we balance virtual relationships and off-line relationships? Is there even such thing as a balance? Not all Facebook users get addicted to it, nor will everyone who does get addicted encounter symptoms identical to mine. Yet I sincerely hope this book will give anyone who finds themselves uncomfortably dependent on social media a no-nonsense look into how I stopped shoveling social media bullshit into my brain, and how I began to sync into my true relationships with myself and with my true friends, no keyboards attached, and how other Facebook addicts can gain the confidence to do it too.

CHAPTER ONE

Status: Rachel Ruff is flirting with Facebook.

*"Heaven, I'm in heaven, and my heart beats
so that I can hardly speak..."*
—*Cheek to Cheek-Irving Berlin*

There have been a few Times in my life when a close friend, a colleague, or a loved one tried to fix me up with Mr. Right. "Oh Rachel, you will love him. He's perfect for you. Everyone loves him and so will you." Then, after much ado, I would hesitatingly accept the blind date, always setting my expectations too high. Not surprisingly, each encounter resulted in a crash and burn outcome. So when one of my dearest friends, Brandon, pushed me to connect with Facebook because he insisted that I would love it, I stubbornly rejected his proposal. To me, Mr. Facebook was my "Mr. Not Right Now."

Brandon introduced me to Facebook in the spring of 2006. Actually, he incessantly nagged me about joining Facebook during the going away party our

CNN colleagues had thrown for me. I was leaving my exciting role as the documentary producer for chief medical correspondent, Dr. Sanjay Gupta, to take a new job in the public relations field and Brandon told me: "You had better get on Facebook in order to keep in touch with me and everyone else you are leaving behind."

I simply rolled my eyes and took another sip of my wine as he rambled on about his love for Facebook. The only social networking site I had ever belonged to was Friendster, from 2003 until 2005, also per Brandon's insistence. But in my opinion, the site wasn't interactive, it was boring, and I'd long since quit using it to send messages or keep up with friends. Personal emails were the norm for my friends to connect with me. I assumed joining Facebook would yield the same blasé results.

A week after the going-away festivities, I started to suffer from a full-blown case of the blues. I had finally finished packing up my belongings in my downtown Atlanta condo to be shipped to my new residence of Washington, DC and all I had to keep myself company during my pity party while labeling boxes that evening were fears and worries about changing careers and moving to a new city.

Dressed in my robe and slippers, I plodded through a hallway of packed and stacked boxes while murmuring to myself, "How can I move away from my CNN family and friends in Atlanta? Heck, I haven't even lived in my new condo here for a year. How will I stay in touch with everyone who I am so used to seeing on a daily basis? What if I don't even like my new job in DC?"

Just then the phone rang, startling me out of my relocation rumination. As soon as I saw Brandon's name pop up on the caller ID, I picked up the phone and tried to sound cheery, "Hey B, what's up?"

Brandon always seemed to sense when I was distressed. Once again, the timing of his call was spot on. "Ruff, how's the packing going?"

Before I could even respond, in his best smarty-pants, sing-song tone, he jested, "I don't see you on Facebook yet. As long as I get to see pictures of you with your big smile and can read your Facebook status updates, I won't feel like you are so far away." After listening to my moaning and groaning about moving for an hour, he ended the call with, "Ruff, I am going to miss you so much. Stop your packing and get your butt on Facebook. I know you, if you don't do it now, you will hit the ground running in DC and tell me you were too busy to sign up."

I promised him that I would join the site solely to keep in touch with him. As we said our good-byes, he laughed and said, "I'm honored that you're joining Facebook for me, but I know that once you join you'll be hooked."

I hung up the phone, put down my packing tape, and typed www.Facebook.com into my idle computer keyboard. "How can you enhance my life?" I whispered to the computer screen as it flashed up the home page with its infamous blue and white Facebook logo. "I'm already active on Linked In, so what more do I need from you? And what does Brandon mean by, "so that he can *see* my status updates?" Isn't my status, that I am moving to DC to become the youngest Vice President at a renowned PR agency, big enough? I'm not ready to make any new changes. What are status updates necessary for anyway? Friendster is dead, Facebook might soon fade away too. How would people even respond to my status updates?"

Just a few weeks prior, I had accepted a senior public relations position in DC as a stepping stone to advance my career, utilizing my "savvy social media skills" as my coworkers coined my online endeavors, which included developing the first CNN medical blog for my boss, Sanjay Gupta, in order to enhance his outreach with his fans. Yet here I was, still completely in the dark about how Facebook would bolster my relationships.

Next to the computer my alarm clock stared back at me flashing midnight. I simply didn't have the energy to sign up for Facebook and start figuring out what promise a Facebook "wall" would reap for me at that moment. "Tomorrow, not right now." I said to myself as I shut down the computer and crawled into bed.

Tomorrow turned into four months later. While I had successfully made the transition from Atlanta to the nation's capital, I had been preoccupied with blooming where I was planted at my new job during my first Washington, DC cherry blossom spring season. Figuring out how to deliver on my lofty promises to get my clients into the media spotlight was my focus. I needed to be able to capitalize on my old

CNN connections, but I had yet to devise a clever and ingenious way of reaching out to my old CNN cronies that would ensure a response. Once I had given my resignation notice to CNN, my security badge was confiscated, meaning I no longer had privileged access through the high security doors of Ted Turner's media empire.

At 21 years old, fresh out of college, I had tirelessly worked my way up the ladder from gopher, as the rookies were nicknamed. Those same broadcaster celebs who had once looked at me askance if the coffee tasted stale or when their scripts were late off the printer now admired my journalistic prowess. The last thing I wanted to do was lose their respect by pestering them for public relations favors to please my demanding clients. I had to formulate a creative and respectable strategy to reach my Rolodex of important CNN contacts for the agency's clients without seeming like a pest.

Ironically, I realized I had become a gopher again, but this time for my new PR bosses, as in, I was instructed to "go for" my CNN contacts. I grimaced with every introduction my boss would make to the new clients I was to represent: "This is Rachel, our new Vice President. She's from CNN. She can get you Larry King, Dr. Gupta, Soledad O'Brien, or Anderson Cooper for your big pharmaceutical convention. We will have Rachel call them today."

In the fast-changing telecommunication world of 2006, rarely did anyone at CNN pick up their direct office phone lines, let alone stop to read my email requests, but I had an aha moment when I realized I could chase them down on Facebook. Though at first I was reluctant to join, I convinced myself that I was signing up in the name of client outreach, and clicked "accept" on the Facebook registration page's button. Voilà! Within seconds I received an email that stated I was now an active Facebook user. In less than an hour I garnered three friend requests from old high school classmates.

Just as I had put Facebook and my dear friend Brandon on the back burner for months, after my first week active on Facebook, I realized I had done the same thing with long-lost friends whose mission was to find me on Facebook. After receiving an additional handful of friend requests, including Brandon's, without even having had a chance to hunt down one person yet to ask to friend me, I felt humbled and honored, yet also very bewildered.

I was shocked that the very same classmates who had once shunned me from sitting at their cafeteria tables for lunch, claiming I was "too pimple-faced and nerdy," were seeking me out on Facebook. Their one-line Facebook friend requests such as, "Jenna wants to friend you on Facebook," were actually more verbiage than they shared with me in high school. I increasingly began to accept all of them with a quick click of the mouse because I delighted in the fact that my Facebook profile picture would be evidence to them that I had finally grown out of the ugly duckling persona I had in high school, as I had so desperately wished I would.

Never in my life had accumulating friends, especially high school ones, been this easy. My pretty blonde
profile picture garnered positive comments from even
the most popular varsity football jocks who had once
barked at me, "Rachel RUFF RUFF is a dog!" Back
then, with my head hung down, I would try to escape
them. But twenty years later, thanks to Facebook, I
was now basking in their digital declarations to me:
"Wow Ruff, you sure didn't turn out looking like a
dog! HOTTIE!!"

Deep inside though, my awkward, pimply-faced,
bean-pole high school self voiced her concerns that
those "cool kids" from school might become suspicious of the profile picture I posted. Would they gossip
via Facebook to the other cool kids that I couldn't be
the same person I appeared to be on my Facebook
page?

Though my account had been activated and I was
quickly reconnecting with my past, I still wasn't completely active with Mr. Facebook. I could only sneak
away and play with him when my work life was quiet.
After all, I was too busy using the site as I originally
intended—as a new and exciting client outreach tool.
I was ahead of my time creating platforms for my
clients to become friends with customers before "fan
pages" were enacted and I quickly became enamored
of Facebook's other charms. Without realizing it, Facebook was becoming both a blessing and a curse.

I became obsessed with trying to boost my own
popularity using the lessons I was teaching my clients about how to sell their businesses and pimp their

products. My online business tactics quickly turned into a selfish strategizing fame game tailored to sell myself to old friends who were now practical strangers. Practical strangers I desperately sought out to fatten my friend list.

Mr. Facebook seemed like a date I accepted so that I would look chic being seen on his arm at an important black tie business gala. Mr. Facebook had given me a chance to show all of those high school jocks and popular girls how I had blossomed into a beautiful swan and I wanted to rub it in. Little did I know, his arm—my Facebook wall—was about to become my crutch: I was about to embark on a steamy affair with this powerful social media stranger I had just met.

Like a teenage girl crazed with the new guy in school whose boyishly charming attributes cause her to cave in to his incessant urges to "go all the way," I soon became obsessed with trying to figure out what sort of limit I should set for my wall. I wondered when I should "put out" for Mr. Facebook by uploading even more sexy and revealing photos of myself. *Dare I post a response back to the flirtatious comments made by bad boys on my wall?* "Meow!" I finally wrote below their comments.

Soon, I began to shift my attention to inspecting others' Facebook pages to compare numbers. *Four hundred friends on the homecoming queen's wall, and I have only fourteen? Not acceptable. She doesn't even look that pretty anymore.*

I also hadn't quite grasped that my "status update" could reveal anything that I wanted it to, for all my friends to see. Not until I began to surf friends' pages and noted their status updates did I start to flirt with the idea of posting my own "Rachel Ruff is: ." Instead, my status profile remained blank for weeks because I wanted to be sure that what I did post would appear suitably clever. While I was always very deft at devising messages for clients' Facebook pages, I felt that I still needed to become fluent in how to craft my own postings to send the right message. I wanted to compose the perfect prose. So many of the updates I saw were boring: "Tina is making spaghetti for dinner."

Finally, two months into Facebook I let my guard down and made it to what I considered "second base" with Mr. Facebook. I slowly typed in my first status update which I considered to be just as dull as the "making spaghetti" status, but I thought was safe enough for me to go ahead and post: "Rachel Ruff is now on Facebook." I held my breath, hit enter, and then covered my eyes. What I discovered, peeking through my fingers at the computer screen just a few minutes later, amazed me. Over half of my forty-plus friends had already clicked the "like" button or replied, "Yay!" and "Great to see you on Facebook finally, Rachel!" Five new friend requests were also waiting for me.

I was enamored with how my blind date seemed to get me noticed. Mr. Facebook's "thumbs up" or "like" button had suddenly become my new "catnip." And I soon found myself hungry for more approval.

Facebook was quickly becoming my new romance as well as my new Rolodex. My friend list was filling up with old pals, colleagues, and CNN anchors, too. Their Facebook friend invitations were helping boost my confidence and increase my value at my firm, not to mention making me look successful and well-connected for my old high school friends. The only group missing from my page was my own kin.

Not one single person in my family had reached out to friend me. But then again, to the best of my knowledge, after having searched for their names in the "find your friends" section, none of my relatives appeared to be on Facebook...*yet*. I was actually kind of relieved as I had always felt like the black sheep in my family and worried how they would judge my wall activity if they were on Facebook. And I was too busy reveling in how wonderful I felt that a herd of Facebook friends were now following me to fret about whether or not my family would become my friends too.

CHAPTER TWO

Status: **Rachel Ruff** is falling in love with Facebook

"What'chu talkin' 'bout Willis?"
—Arnold from Different Strokes

WiTh each new friend requesT i received, Facebook not only brought another acquaintance to my recently developed Facebook wall, but also a bright smile to my face. There were times when a long-lost pal would post about a race for which she was training, a diet goal, or a charity fundraising initiative, and the posts brought me much joy from reading about their ambitions.

Surfing on long lost girlfriends' walls, I noticed that several of them were rallying for another cause: they were trying to get pregnant. One particular afternoon in 2007, almost a year after joining Facebook, I stumbled upon an old high school friend's profile update as soon as it popped up on the recently created Facebook live news feed. Ramona had uploaded an ultrasound image of her baby with a post that read, "Just returned home from my first trimester ob/gyn prenatal appointment!" How fun to discover that someone whom I hadn't seen since I was a kid, was now expecting a little one.

Her picture told a million words. Family and friends who had kept up with her posts in the months past had read about how arduous the act of trying to conceive a child had been for her. In my opinion, her constant "Hubby and I are going to make a baby tonight!" alerts were prime examples of Facebook over-sharing. But then again, who was I to judge? I was beginning to embark on over-sharing on Facebook too, like the response I posted below her baby news. "SO happy for you Ramona! But I sure don't want any rug rats!" The posts of jubilation below her ultrasound pic seemed to trail on forever. I may not have envied her for becoming a mommy, but I childishly envied how many comments she acquired from her exciting news.

Sadly, I also recall when another old high school girlfriend's Facebook update stated, "Miscarried for the second time this year." By sharing the devastating news via her status update, she garnered an overwhelming response of kind and thoughtful messages.

Some might consider her posting to be TMI or too much information, which was exactly how I felt. But for her, perhaps TMI stood for "This Mommy's Inconsolable." I believe she felt the need to post about her pain on Facebook for our support, which she got. A few months later, when her Facebook status read, "Third time's the charm!" we all comprehended exactly what she meant. Once her baby was born, her own profile picture was never seen again. Instead, she used her baby photos as her Facebook image, which irked me. "Had she lost her identity? Why can't she post her own face?"

But who was I to talk? I was in the throes of conceiving a strategy to generate new Facebook friends, not to cultivate friendships, but to add their names to my wall and boast of my association with the movers and shakers of DC. When I made new connections at grand Embassy dinner parties, DC fundraising events, and swanky clubs I wanted all of them to become my Facebook friends.

"Hi, I'm Rachel Ruff. Friend me on Facebook" was my new introduction at galas. But when I began to worry that my introductions would be forgotten or my business card lost, I changed my socializing strategy to "What is your last name? I'll find you on Facebook!"

In order to doubly ensure that I could connect with those who were still in the digital Dark Ages and hadn't yet jumped on the Facebook bandwagon, I would say, "Make sure you join Facebook. I'll email you a friend request!" Then I'd spend the rest of the night chanting their names and emails in my head so as not to forget after the party was over. Sometimes I would even dash into the bathroom to write the more unusual or difficult to spell names on a cocktail napkin so I could friend request them as soon as I got home. (In 2007, a Facebook app was not yet available for cell phones. When it did become available, I thought of how much easier my life would have been.)

Just as I had taken blogging to a new level at CNN

by drawing viewers into online live chat discussions with Dr. Gupta, I soon began convincing every one of my clients and colleagues to join Facebook. I ensured them that by making the site their new best friend they would quickly attract new followers while simultaneously strengthening the bond with their existing clients and customers.

Once again, I was ahead of my time, as there was no such thing as a Facebook fan page in 2007. When the social utility site began to gain membership momentum as big businesses like my clients caught on, a new media platform was born. People began to use Facebook not only for finding friends but to find "fans" for their businesses and products. I was thrilled because the advertising revolution on Facebook meant I had an excuse to spend even more time getting to know Mr. Facebook during my company's business hours.

Here's how a typical brainstorm meeting at my firm went at the time: "Rachel, we need you to help us get XYZ pharmaceuticals in the social media spotlight." To which I would instantly respond, "Well, do they have a page on Facebook?" A silent pause would engulf the room. From the other end of the mahogany boardroom table, the firm's president would then remark, as if I had just made a brilliant discovery, like Christopher Columbus sailing the Internet blue, "No, they do not! Rachel, please start building their Facebook page immediately."

My newfound and effective advertising exposure tactics for our clients were working so well that my boss nicknamed me "The Idea Factory." Earning a six-figure salary in the name of social media could never be better. That is, until the economy took a hit and the agency's business started to decline. Thankfully however, our social media department was the only branch that was being allocated funding due to our newfound digital client strategy. My team was greatly saving the firm as well as our clients millions in advertising dollars by forgoing the traditional and expensive media buys that included television appearances, newspaper features, magazines spreads, etc. We were being heralded for using our fresh tactics online.

Gone were the days of setting up fancy studio arrangements to record a Public Service Announcement for clients. One P.S.A. could run up to ten thousand dollars or more in production costs. And the labor costs to vet them out to television stations and newspapers doubled the expenses. Plus, we were at the mercy of the networks to decide whether they even wanted to broadcast our messages. Risking all that money with no guarantee for exposure seemed like double trouble to me. Yet convincing some of my old-school bosses and especially my clients that "tweeting and uploading videos would save them thousands of dollars and simultaneously attract thousands of eyeballs was even more arduous.

At an office-wide strategy meeting one morning, I blurted out to the same boardroom of executives who once gave me eager nods of approval, "All you need to do is entrust me with just a few hours of my billing time and a small hand-held camera and we will be good to go." My boss looked at me as if I had two heads. "To shoot interviews and campaign videos for our biggest clients? Do you know what you are risking?"

"Yep, losing the agency another client and my own job, for sure." She said she would think about it.

A few hours later, she appeared at my office, standing in the doorway with a grim look upon her face and her hands on her hips. "Fine, just know I am not going to save your ass if it flops." And off I went on my cyber-sphere adventure with only adrenaline and a little Cannon HD hand-held to aid me. I was a one-man band shooting interviews in clients' offices and outdoors without the aid of fancy lighting or elaborate studio sets. A canopy of trees and the D.C. monuments served as my aesthetically pleasing backdrops. Heck, our social media team even borrowed cute babies from our friends to save on modeling fees when shooting Facebook and YouTube videos for our clients' baby products.

Rather than sending the finished videos out to news organizations, I simply hit "upload" and presto; the videos were live. Able to be found by Internet surfers all across the world on YouTube, Facebook, etc. Our "Who is the Cutest Kitty" campaign reaped in 2,000 or more hits a day. Heck, I didn't even have to pay the bloggers who found our campaigns and shared them on their heavily trafficked websites. Now all I have to do is focus on improving my Facebook page's popularity in order to reap the same results I'm bringing to my clients, I mused.

"Mr. Not Right Now" had become my morning, noon, and night as I was constantly discovering new ways to make him a positive part of my life. He was my rock in solidifying client support, connecting me to friends, and protecting my job security. He was my playground, filled with a wealth of friends' fun recommendations, new songs to listen to, recipes to try, and exciting events to attend. Mr. Facebook and I were riding high. And I was also feeling the rush from the newfound portal I discovered to share my messages, to show myself to the world.

I truly thought Facebook was an arranged date finally gone right. Never in my life had going on a blind date felt as thrilling as when I logged onto Facebook for the first time. I had always kept my expectations low on dates. And if and when I did accept a blind date, my safety net was, "I'll take my car, and he can take his. I'll meet him there." Then I would sniff out the guy to see if I deemed him worthy of pursuing a relationship. If I deemed him unworthy, I would quickly lurch my heart and my car in reverse in order to escape before he got too close.

But as soon as I locked eyes with Facebook's beautiful blue screen, I drove myself straight into a wall, my Facebook wall that is, to sit back and read the constant influx of fresh updates rolling in as well as the gratifying responses sent to me. I was hooked because I loved the idea that people might be just as immersed in virtually looking at me as I was at them. According to go-gulf.com in a February 2012 report, an average Facebook user spent around 7 hours, 45 minutes and

49 seconds per month on Facebook. I guess I was not the "normal" user, because I began spending 46 minutes per hour, for seven hours a day on Facebook in a five-day work week during 2007. Even scarier, I was almost fooled into believing that I had an actual social life. Visiting friends' walls on the weekends often sidetracked me from attending social outings that I had previously committed to. I even began to wish that inter-office memos would just come into my Facebook feed so that I didn't have to keep logging out to check on my work emails and see if any new projects had come my way.

After crashing and getting stalled on Facebook for hours, rather than going to a repair shop I simply remained parked against my wall, a spot specially reserved just for me, to revel in a superfluous magnitude of graffiti and self-gratification laced across my Facebook masterpiece. There should have been a disclaimer for anyone who visited my wall reading, "Everything you don't need to know and more. Free parking!"

CHAPTER THREE

Status: Rachel Ruff is a lady on the street, but a freak on her wall

"The greatest trick the Devil ever pulled was convincing the world he didn't exist."
—*Kint from* The Usual Suspects

On Typical WashingTOn, dc weekday mOrnings, my Type A self was K Street bound. The busy metropolis thoroughfare was once dubbed the "road to riches" because of the multitude of powerful lobbyists, influencers, and think tanks that bustled about the bureaucracy. But my grand visions soon turned sour during the dolorous ending of 2007, thanks to the demise of our client list.

With a global recession impending, our firm's business had slowed dramatically because corporations who contracted us were cutting their PR and advertising budgets first. Our office began laying people off at an increasingly rapid rate. Luckily, the agency was holding onto me, presumably in their hopes new business would soon spring up and they could utilize my resourceful social media skills.

Sadly, my pre-occupation with my Facebook page was growing unhealthy because of the extra time I had on my hands from lack of work. I no longer had client projects to distract me from going to Facebook to pass the hours. *If only the agency had some new projects so my idle hands would be too busy to play in the devil's workshop*, I ruminated.

One morning, I was decked in Converse sneakers rather than my designer heels because I had no client meetings to dress to impress. As I fought my way off the crowded 8:00 a.m. metro train, I realized that the inelegance of my rush hour routine was beginning to feel exhausting and unexciting. *What the hell am I fighting to get to the office on time for? To be stuck at a desk under fluorescent lighting for eight hours? All I have at work is my Facebook friends to keep me company.*

With each new morning I arrived in an office resembling a ghost town, I would increasingly sense the presence of a little angel and a devil at my desk devoid of to-do lists. The angel would perch on my right shoulder and sweetly but sadly greet me. While she looked down upon my computer screen as I logged on to Facebook, she would whisper things like, "Rachel, what if a coworker screen grabs that photo of you in the bikini with the furry snow boots and sends it on to your boss?" and "Your friend Trish just posted a comment about how much fun she had partying with you the other night. Didn't you call in sick that day? Please delete the note. It's for your own good." I wanted to shush her but I couldn't, and her whispers of warning seemed to be growing louder and more frequent. I wasn't actually hearing voices, but there was a definite inner dialogue between my good instincts and my bad ones.

It was like having an angel and a devil in my head making comments about the way I should live my life. The combination of my increasing Facebook paranoia interlaced with anxiety regarding my job security was not helping pacify the voices either. I became suspicious that the angel might be warning me that I had a Facebook addiction. I reluctantly acknowledged to myself that I preferred to search for new friends to add to my Facebook wall, rather than using my downtime to search for a new job online. I started to wonder if I was becoming a closet Facebook junkie just itching for more and more friends' approval. I used to be able to justify my Facebook usage hours by blaming it on client research, now the excuse was no longer valid.

In the name of virtue, I would log out of Facebook and work on compiling a list of companies online who were looking for social media executives to hire. Predictably, just minutes later, I'd sense a tap on my left shoulder and hear the devil's voice taunting me, "Yo, Ruff, you need to log back in and figure out how Simone got so skinny. Check out those beach photos of her again and see if she looks like she's had plastic surgery. Post some of your low-cut ball gown pictures from the Embassy party and beat her out while you are at it."

As I tried to think of what in the hell I could post

as an exciting status to please the devil, I had a moment of clarity. I realized the old "Idea Factory" girl was quickly becoming a Facebook freak. I went from building beautiful and exciting new Facebook pages for my clients to building my own self-gratifying social media sweatshop. Why did I feel the need to impress my Facebook friends? Why did I feel the need to open my page to the noisy traffic of male friends I didn't really know who I'd lured onto my wall? My Facebook flirting had completely gotten out of control. For instance, when a cute friend of a friend of mine would friend request me after seeing a tagged photo with my name below the picture on his friend's wall, I would instantly click accept. Then the guy would suddenly become my new virtual best friend and our superficial relationship would flourish by mutually posting witticisms to each other's walls, asking where the hippest parties were going to be in DC that weekend, etc. Worries about "stranger danger" never occurred to me. I craved drama. Excitement. Anything to pass the time at my desk.

Sadly, the friendship I really needed to cultivate was with myself, but I simply couldn't find any true love within me to share with myself. The more I surfed on Facebook comparing myself to others, the more envious I became of my more popular friends and celebrities. Where was the young woman who once proudly puffed out her chest as she strutted down K Street with dreams and lofty ideas bursting from her brain? Why did she switch gears and become a "post-itute," uploading herself in scantily clad clothes and loitering on others' walls to attract an audience?

Perhaps because I subconsciously wished to become the superstar I had so yearned to be at CNN. I had tried again and again to become an on-camera reporter but I always got "You are too gifted as a writer, we need your producer talents." I think I compensated by using my Facebook page as my anchor desk in order to throw myself into the social media limelight.

Tomorrow will be better I would tell myself after a case of the Facebook blues would hit. And when I felt drained and paranoid that I did have a Facebook addiction after putting in a full day of Facebook surfing, I would head home determined to prove my conscience wrong. Good intentions to spend my evening painting or listening to music and burn new iTunes releases only resulted in posting YouTube links to the songs on Facebook. Rather than actually listening to the music, I was listening for the beep of a new Facebook notification to reveal that my post had been noticed. A bad day then became a good day when someone "listened" to me.

And the vicious cycle would begin all over again. I began to relate to the character played by Bill Murray in "Groundhog Day" who asked, "What would you do if you were stuck in one place and every day was exactly the same, and nothing that you did mattered?" I was stumped. With each new day, I hoped that I could escape the mundane and for once be able to muster enough stamina to keep from getting high on Facebook as soon as I entered the office. My work life had become so blasé. Punch in, punch out.

Log in to Facebook. Log out. The same bosses who had once encouraged me to work overtime to build out our clients' platforms began to urge me to step away from my desk (and Facebook) to go outside for a walk. Their advice would have been more acceptable if it didn't conflict with my Facebook lunch meetings. Noon was the posting primetime for my East Coast friends who were actually busy at work. A time when they could update their postings and even better, a time when they could catch up with my updates and comment on them.

On the bright side, when I followed bosses' orders and took a break to pick up my favorite garlicky gyro from a street vendor, I no longer had to worry about mouthwash because I'd head right back up to the quiet office and lock the door from my colleagues, and settle in at my desk to get a big welcome back kiss from my Mr. Facebook. None of my shortcomings, including bad breath or avoiding a meet-up with friends face to face, seemed to short circuit his love for me. According to Mr. Facebook, the old adage "a friend to all is a friend to none" was bullshit. I was brainwashed into believing that a Facebook friend to all, *is* a friend to all.

Come sunny afternoons, I would do twenty minutes of posting and then force myself to get outside and walk around the mall looking up at the quotations inscribed on the FDR Memorial stone walls hoping they would speak to me. One day a Roosevelt quote jumped out at me: "No country however rich, can afford the waste of its human resources. Demoralization caused by vast unemployment is our greatest extravagance. Morally, it is the greatest menace to our social order."

Yet the wall's demoralization meaning took on a different connotation in my mind. As soon as I got back to my desk, I surfed the Facebook walls of some of the last demoralized survivors in our office to see what they were voicing on their Facebook pages in the hopes their words would inspire me with a clever update to post as my status and improve my "social order."

One afternoon I came across a coworker's update, "Carrie is volunteering at the Red Cross." But her update didn't inspire me, in fact, it pissed me off. *Why am I so upset that she is doing volunteer work?* The angel startled me by answering in a stern tone, "Because, Rachel, unlike you, she is doing *something besides Face-booking.*" I simply couldn't surrender to the truth that I had nothing to give, nothing to share. Dumbfounded I sat there trying to brush my angel of annoyance from my shoulder.

I entertained the idea that I should volunteer somewhere so I could post about my charity work like Carrie had. How could I have made the time and effort though?

After all, I was too busy volunteering anything anyone wanted to know, yet nothing of much significance to my Facebook wall. Was it doing any good for anyone? Was posting doing anything good for me either? No, not really but that didn't stop me from posting the comment, "Well GFY!!! ;-) xo" below Carrie's posting.

My "GFY" wasn't an acronym for "Good for you" though. I snidely meant "Go F@&*%" Yourself. The desire to become a Facebook sensation was turning me into a Facebook frenemy. Until I would awake the next morning to witness my posting and feel my morning-after guilt.

This relationship with Mr. Facebook is getting too intense for me. My God, how could I go crazy on sweet Carrie? Post something really, really nice to her wall to cancel out your negative energy...

I sloppily typed "BTW when's the next Red Cross event? I want 2 sign up with-u!!!"

I sighed with relief when Carrie's big-hearted comment came back to me a few minutes later: "YOU ARE THE BEST RACHIE! SUN. AM. I'll pick u up @ 9:00!" All day long our conversation received a handful of thumbs ups. I was wildly overjoyed, almost feeling lightheaded from the responses to our good deeds.

Did I ever end up joining Carrie that Sunday to volunteer? Heck no. But that wasn't my intention. My intention was to score admiration with Facebookers and my mission was accomplished. But I was headed for damnation. As former Secretary of State Madeleine Albright once said, "there's a special place in hell for women who don't help other women."

The devil patted me on the back and hissed, "So, is Facebook no longer bringing you any pleasure? Go ahead and quit then, my dear. It seems like that angel of yours never explained to you that spreading little white lies on Facebook can sometimes bring you even closer to your friends. I bet she never informed you that other people lie on Facebook too. A LOT. You are *not* addicted to Facebook. You *are* simply passionate. Now get back to work. Hurry up and post to Carrie's wall that you were sick on Sunday."

The devil in me had reignited my desperate desire for approval. *Please look at my smiling face and like my lofty updates*, was the silent plea I had interlaced within my posts and my pictures. When I'd get a "Nice one, RR" comment as a response to my witty wall post-ings, I was like a digital doggie who had been inces-santly wagging my tail, eagerly awaiting someone to pet me as a reward for freshly dumping doo-doo onto my wall. No one ever scolded me or spanked me with a newspaper, as they should have done for my own good.

My heart was on a teeter-totter with Mr. Facebook. Some days I was up, other days I was down. Always struggling to find the balance. Especially on the days when I felt he wasn't there to support and pay atten-tion to me. On those days I would come crashing down. *Why doesn't he put out for me as I do for him?* If I didn't get the recognition I felt I deserved, I would feel like a failure and retreat and log out. But within minutes I would brush myself off and hop back on the social media see-saw.

As a result, I began to get increasingly involved with my quasi-boyfriend and lazy about cultivating my real-life friendships. I was still not yet sure how to attract the magnitude of fans, aka friends I yearned to have. When Facebook hit the high millions in members, I cringed at Mr. Facebook's friends as I compared them to mine. "Only six hundred friends? Shit, I want six-thousand."

Face to face relationships began to take a permanent backseat as I was on a mad quest to build my friend list instead. For instance, if a friend posted he/she was going into surgery, I'd post "Praying for a speedy recovery for you" and then quickly click over to my latest and greatest new guy pal's wall to engage in some flirty and fun banter. What happened to the old Rachel Ruff who would drop everything to get to the hospital to be by a true friend's side? Now all I had to do was stop at their wall for a mere ten seconds. I even started failing to respond to friends' voicemail messages and canceling coffee dates. I preferred to percolate new wall posts instead.

Thankfully, I did dredge up the humanitarian in me to log off of Facebook, and pick up the phone to call my friend Angela a few times during her last days. Earlier that year, Angela, whom I had been close to for over ten years, even before Facebook existed, was given a stage four cancer diagnosis and a prediction of just eight months to live. I was still present enough to send a slew of handwritten cards and care packages to my dear friend.

There she was, trapped in a body ridden with cancer cells, fighting for a cancer cure with the top oncologists in the United States treating her. While I, her terminally-ill Facebook and real life friend basically purveyed to her, "Hi, I want you to know that whatever suffering you are going through, I'm here to read about it on Facebook." The sicker Angela became the best I could do was post encouragement to her wall. Her diagnosis had been haunting and I was childishly hiding behind Mr. Facebook's coattails rather than accepting the brevity of her situation and truly being there for her. Finding new friends to accept me was my coping and escape mechanism.

During my last phone conversation with Angela she whispered to me, "Rachel, I want you to meet a great man. One who loves you, one who adores you, for everything you are."

A few weeks later, one cold and snowy December evening in DC, my friend passed away. Beside myself from the loss, the next morning, I was still unable to fully accept that Angela, forty-seven years young, was gone. I clicked and re-clicked on her Facebook page that had become a memorial site, and the overflow of our friends' condolences acted as a confirmation to me that she really was in heaven now. I posted not even one memorial comment to her wall, I felt that would be too impersonal. For once, I didn't want attention. I wanted my friend back.

Forcing myself to get out of the house, I shuffled through the dirty snow and into my favorite grunge musician-populated coffee shop while clutching tightly to my laptop. I was looking to plug into Mr. Facebook for comfort and to mourn her passing with a warm cup of coffee, but the preppy, sock-less Italian shoe-wearing man I was seated next to kept trying to strike up a conversation with me.

Geez. The last thing on my mind is to find love over a latte, so quit trying to bug me, I thought. Hi, "Karl with a K" as you so cleverly introduced yourself, nice to meet you. But can't you see I'm busy on Facebook? I'd need to inspect your Facebook profile first anyway, Mr. Sock-less. I desperately wished "Karl with a K" would just pack up and leave.

After three hours of reluctantly making what I deemed pointless conversation, Karl, who I'd learned was in town from Colorado, finally closed his laptop and mustered up the courage to ask me if he could take me to lunch.

As I watched Karl nervously loop his cashmere scarf around his neck and button up his coat, I pondered his request. Hesitating, because while I was ravenous and having a hard time turning down a free lunch, I decided to forgo his offer. "I think you've taken up enough of my time," I said. Then, a little chagrined about being so curt, I added, "Just find me on Facebook. I'm Rachel. Rachel Ruff."

He told me that he couldn't look me up on Facebook because he wasn't on the site, and I was nonplussed. *How in the hell am I going to be able to sniff him out and make sure he's not some kind of a weirdo? After all, who in the world isn't on Facebook?! Glad I didn't accept his offer.*

"Karl with a K" was an unlikely candidate for me to pursue for a number of reasons: 1) He was wearing loafers and no socks in the middle of winter. 2) He was the most clean-cut guy in a room filled with long-haired hipster types. 3) He was from out of town. 4) He was not on Facebook. 5) He was fifteen years my senior.

Hesitantly, I handed over my business card. After he left, I Googled him over and over again. I soon discovered that even an online profile of Mr. Sock-less was impossible to find. All I could deduce was that Karl was the same age as Angela had been, and was without any Internet presence except for a blurb on a charity website noting him for his generous donation to a triathlon event in the name of cancer research.

Heck, while meeting this stranger had distracted me from my grief, in the back of my mind I couldn't help but wonder if Angela had planted him there. Out of faith, I went so far as to Facebook message a friend of mine in the police force, to pull up a criminal background check on him which came up clean. Ironically, Karl was the one who should have gotten an investigator to pull up what a web-wacko I was!

So there I sat, lost online and lost in love and bereft of my dear Angela. Preferring to spend all of my time with my Mr. Facebook, engrossed in my deep and dark social media secret, rather than accept a lunch date with a real man. Somehow Facebook had become my crack gone sideways and everything in between.

CHAPTER FOUR

Status: Rachel Ruff hopes what happens in Vegas, stays off Facebook

"Some days you get the bear, other days the bear gets you."
—Old English Proverb

as The cOld and grey winTer dragged On, I remained confined indoors and snuggled up by the fireplace with Mr. Facebook. I sensed our relationship seemed to need the click of the refresh button. I had run out of sassy, sexy statuses to fill out after the "is" following my name. "Who *is* Rachel Ruff to him anymore?" *Rachel Ruff is: a "has been" who is spending her days in captivity by obsessing over what the hell she should write as her status update. That's who she is.*

Rachel Ruff is: *hoping she keeps her job?* Nah.
Rachel Ruff is: *drinking a bottle of cheap wine and drunk-Facebook-ing tonight?* Negative.
Rachel Ruff is: *down one Facebook friend because she croaked?*
No. No. NO!

Rachel Ruff is: *a Debby Downer.* Perfecto.

And then one morning, I awoke to discover something remarkable. Mr. Facebook had re-ignited my passion for him by removing the "is" after my name. I felt as if he had finally taken a step forward in the feelings department of our relationship. He endearingly took me by the hand and removed the humble little promise ring from my finger, liberating me to say anything.

The change in Mr. Facebook's status took my level of devotion to him from like to downright lust. My status updates soon became an ostentatious social media shit-show.

Back in my early Facebook days, the "Rachel Ruff is:" updates were simple and sweet. Here are a few examples.

Rachel Ruff is:
"working on a new client project!"
"planting tulips"
"looking forward to the Labor Day weekend"
"heading to the rooftop pool at Heather's"
"sick with strep throat"
"catering for a big event"
"having a hard time breathing. Broken ribs."
"decorating her Christmas tree."
"training for her 4th marathon. 26.2 miles baby!"

But once the social media site dropped the "is" after our profile name headers in December of 2007, claiming the change would give users more freedom to post anything in their status updates, including their present, past, or future, I eagerly enhanced my status notifications and along the way, began to tarnish my image with reckless abandon. "Rachel Ruff is:" suddenly became, "Rachel Ruff is, was, can, could, wants to be, or say: anything!" Here are a few examples of my new—and what I considered improved—status updates.

Rachel Ruff:
"hopes they serve hot dogs in heaven"
"wishes everyone a happy 4:20 on 4/20!"
"is PMS-ing"
"Lah-laa-laa loves making snowmen"
"has a dirty job to do tonight. Cleaning the latrines."
"is addicted to Starbucks gingerbread lattes. Crack in a cup!" "needs some beer to wash down her french fries and dirty nachos." "Goooooooo University of Florida Gators! Alabama SUX!"
"Has a house for sale. Fiancé foreclosure, anyone interested?"

I also became a quote whore. But I never attributed the quotes to dear Mary Poppins, Chris Farley, Uma Thurman, Sir Mix Alot, Shakespeare, and a gazillion others.

"Supercalifragilisticexpialidocious"
"Well la-dee-frickin-da"
"I said God Damn! God Damn!"
"Likes big butts and I cannot lie."
"Grapple them to thy soul with hoops of steel."

It wasn't enough to post any old thing; I needed to make a splash. To be freaking impressive. A stand-out among all statuses. That was my mission on Facebook; my digital dharma. Which got me high from the throngs of thumbs ups. I had completely stripped down into what I considered my new and improved social media slutty self, while ashamedly covering up the digital darling I had once been coined by my superiors.

Come April, my status updates were in full bloom. The morning after I flew back from running the Nashville Rock N' Roll marathon, I made yet another humdinger posting. I had suffered a scary brush with hyponatremia during the race, which is the state of over-hydrating one's self that causes an imbalance of sodium in the body and can prove fatal if left untreated.

I wanted to post about my experience on my wall, yet I felt my Facebook friends might not be able to fathom (or even believe) the dire circumstance I had put myself in if I simply posted, "Rachel Ruff survived hyponatremia."

I didn't want to be a buzzkill. So instead of broadcasting my near death experience on Facebook, I shared something even gorier but funnier which I figured would reap even more comments for me: *"Rachel Ruff: just woke up in a bed of bloody sheets. Lost my big toenail. Damn marathon."*

Sure enough, the pain I felt from my bloody stump was almost forgotten once I saw how many people sent me love via their comments over my misfortune.

"Poor dear!", "Gross, a bloody toe?!", "No more pedi-cures!" *Brilliant,* I thought to myself as I realized my wall had suddenly become heavily trafficked, thanks to my bloody toe.

After that voyeuristic victory, I became a loose cannon of TMIs, something I had snickered at others for doing when they posted about their adorable little baby's potty training success or a new word their little tyke just learned. Yet I ultimately became the one with a bad case of "digital diarrhea of the mouth."

Another toxic trend emerged as I willfully began to lie and embellish my posts in order to get high. I simply needed to garner more digital kitty crack. And I don't mean by licking up a few little likes below my "charity" comment on Trish's wall. No, these were complete and utter bullshit injections to my wall. Here are a few fibs I posted that spring in order to get my buzz on:

> *"Broke both my legs last night, working from home today."*
> *"Will be spending the summer in Alsace."*
> *"Hung out with Rob Lowe and John Kerry last night in Georgetown"*

While I seemed to have no hesitation about what I'd post as a status update, I was never comfortable shar-ing my relationship status as many of my friends did. After all, where was the "flavor of the month" button which would be the most accurate choice? There was an "it's complicated" option I could choose to describe my relationship status, but my relationships were far more than that to me.

I would have had to wipe my status slate clean and update my "relationship" graph perhaps more often than some people take showers! "In a Relationship" to "Single" to "In a Relationship" to "Engaged" to "Single" to "Married." And yes, that was the exact order, in just two years, of my relationship track record... it was *kinda* complicated, to say the least.

Plus I had seen many friends change their relationship status after a break-up only to suffer further from an influx of "What happened?" or "Are you okay?" and some even worse remarks like "Who broke up with who?!"

Back in the pre-Facebook days of the 1990s, my girlfriends and I would plan a night on the town to cheer a newly single gal pal. Worse case scenario, one of us had to drive over to a friend's ex's apartment to pick up her CDs or favorite T-shirt. But after the dawn of Facebook, my friends and I were usually too busy untagging the 1,458 pictures of our significant others and us as a couple in an effort to move on and/or heal. I once had a friend who was irate about a nasty split up, even though she was the one to end it, because she discovered he had changed his Facebook status from "in a relationship" to "single" before she did. My friend's wall was bombarded with commiserating messages from well-wishers because everyone assumed her ex had broken up with her.

Facebook breakups are in no way satisfying because the broken up couple's pictures are still fully intact and live on in cyberspace. I missed the days of the "burn the boy" parties which I would host to cheer my broken hearted girlfriends. We would tear our ex's photos into shreds and toss them into the crackling fireplace as we shared our, "Oh no, he didn't do that! Or did he!?" stories.

Gone are the days of using sharp objects and fire for breakup therapy. Someone should create an app called "The relationship ripper" where you can have couples' pictures photoshopped in Facebook photo albums to show the split!

But I stuck to my guns with Mr. Facebook because, *we were not going to break up! He was going to make me a superstar.* Especially because he seemed like such a perfect yet unexpected match for me. Making me, once a teenage wallflower, feel like my wall was proof that I was important, popular, and pretty.

Upon entering college in 1993, I had desperately wanted to be in a sorority, but when I was accepted into Delta Delta Delta, I couldn't afford the dues so I had to drop out. In doing so, I got dumped by a very handsome and popular fraternity boy who stated to me that he "only dated within the Greek system."

With Mr. Facebook, I didn't have to pay any sorority monthly dues or insurance to belong, all I had to do was "put out" in order to become whoever I needed to be to those guys who had once belittled or dumped me in high school and college. The irony was, the tri-Delts had been given a slogan nickname of "Try Delt, everyone else has." So in a sense, I became a "Try Ruff, everyone else has on Facebook!"

Despite my loyalty to Mr. Facebook and my flavor-of-the-month status, someone did come along to compete for my affections. The shy stranger from Denver had finally reached out to the popular Facebook girl from the coffee shop, who was lonely in real life after having just suffered another break up.

Via email Karl wrote to me, *"Hey Rachel, I'm due for another visit to DC in a few weeks. Can I call to see when you are free? I'd like to take you out for dinner."* I dully replied two days later, "Sure. Here is my number." When he called the next day, I answered, "Karl? Karl who?" *Oh shit, it's the coffee shop guy.* Dinner? *Dinner would be too much,* I figured a happy hour quick meet up would be better. He obliged.

Later that month, I begrudgingly put down my laptop and joined him for a few appetizers. The date went well, and I offered to take him to an exhibit at the Smithsonian the next day. Still wary of the non-social media user, when I awoke I quickly regretted my offer. For the next two mornings, the unassuming westerner persistently called to see when we were going to hit the museum. But rather than return his calls, I avoided him. *Sorry buddy, but if your method of communication isn't through Facebook, then I ain't reachable. Why in the hell did I ever suggest a museum date anyway? Dumb idea. Did I really think that by spending more time with him I'd be able to coax him onto Facebook? He probably has a girlfriend he doesn't want me to find out about and that's why he is staying off Facebook.*

"Get over it, girlfriend, you've already got a boy-friend" the devil teased back. He wasn't any help so I turned to the Facebook name search field to prove the devil wrong. I thought my social media skills of persuasion like I used on my clients could make Karl come hither to Mr. Facebook and me. But no such luck. *Why doesn't Karl want to join now that he knows I'm on it? Then he can peek into my life and see what I am up to? If I'm dating anyone?* I groused to myself for weeks over Karl's non-existent Facebook wall. A long-distance relationship with a guy in Colorado already seemed like a deal-breaker, and if I couldn't scope him out on Facebook, I just couldn't see the point of pursuing the connection. I went right on stubbornly ignoring Karl's phone calls.

But he remained persistent. One month later, the phone rang while my best friend Trish was over baking a cake with me for a Memorial weekend party we were hosting that evening. She looked down to see Karl's name on the caller ID. "Pick up the damn phone, Rachel. For God sakes, this Karl guy might be just as f'd up as you in the relationship department." Glaring back at her I replied, "You think I'm going to fall for a guy I can't spy on? I need to see who this coffee shop stranger really is, if he's married, if he's a dad, some kind of pervert etc. but I can't. Can you believe he's *not on Facebook?*"

Apparently, my argument was not compelling enough for Trish. She quickly hit the "return call" button and shoved the phone to my ear. He answered, a bit taken aback that I actually returned his phone call for once. I nervously blurted, "Guess what! We're in the same city." He replied confused, "You're in Denver?" "No, I'm in DC! I thought you were coming out here again." Another long pause from Karl. And then

I recalled why he must be perplexed by my responses. I wanted to put my foot in my mouth! Oh shit. I got a voicemail from him about a month before saying he would be in DC again for the Memorial weekend and that he wanted to take me out to dinner so I lied and told him I'd be out of town. Slyly, I had returned his call at 6 a.m. EST the next day, assuming he would probably be asleep and the call would go straight to voicemail. "Hi, Karl. Have fun in DC. I'll be in Florida so unfortunately we can't meet up." Click.

And then he shyly and sweetly mustered into the receiver, "Rachel I was only coming out to see *you*." "Karl, I feel terrible. I'm so sorry and I'm so honored. I was being standoffish to you because I am scared of getting my heart broken in another relationship. Plus I don't do long distance relationships. My best friend, here sitting next to me, convinced me to call you back. I'm so glad I did!"

I could barely hear him on the other line because Trish was jumping for joy and cheering and *embarrassing the crap out of me*. "Well, there's one problem." Karl said in his thick country accent. "I decided to give up on the girl and I cancelled my ticket. I'm in the car headed home to Kansas to hang out with my brother. But I'm going to turn around now to the airport and see if my seat is still available." Later I learned he had exceeded speeds of 100 mph to get him across the Kansas border in order to catch the flight. Breathless, he boarded just as the flight attendant was shutting the gate.

Thank God I listened to Trish and let my guard

down. Our weekend together was amazing. After the party, we caught a cab to my place and sat upon my kitchen counter sharing our life stories until the birds began chirping. Looking into his eyes, I realized there was something special, almost magical between us. I realized the non-Facebook issue I once had with Karl was not a deal breaker at all. In fact, I found his reserved nature to be sort of boyishly charming. *He's just a very quiet and introspective guy. Opposites attract is right.*

Just as the coffee shop stranger now turned my potential prince charming was leaving for the National airport, he asked me to visit him in Denver the weekend of June the 6th. Sadly, I explained that I was heading to Vegas for my sister's 30th birthday party that weekend to which he quickly responded, "Vegas is just a quick plane ride away for me." I said "Okay."

In "Sin City" that Sunday, just three dates later, I said "yes" to him again but with much more passion, inside of The Heavenly Bliss Wedding Chapel on June 8, 2008. I walked down the aisle, not in a wedding gown, but wearing a hot pink t-shirt, white clamdiggers, and flip-flops. Neither one of us can pinpoint exactly how we "just knew" while making the spontaneous decision over breakfast to elope just an hour before our flights were to take me back to DC and him home to Denver. We simply acted on our intuition, not on alcohol, as some might assume. And we missed our Sunday afternoon flights home.

However sweet Karl, my sock-less, social-media-less stranger and I, his social media spouse, couldn't just float away to la-la land while sipping bubbly champagne to kick off our marriage. Well, at least for one night we did. We checked into the extravagant Wynn hotel's honeymoon suite where the staff catered to us like we were just crowned king and queen.

Reality set in the next morning. And our whirlwind love story morphed into more of a nightmare. Tears started streaming down my face and my hands were shaking. Not because I had made the wrong decision, but because of the potential Facebook fallout. Foolishly the night before, I had sent a few cell phone elopement pictures to just a few of our best friends. Next I left my boss a voicemail stating that I was in the middle of a family emergency and that I would be back to work a day late. The only thing I didn't do was call my mother, because I knew she would be outraged. All it would take to spark a web wildfire was for one of my friends to post the photos I had sent on Facebook with a comment like "Congrats Rachel and Karl!" or "So that's what happens in Vegas Baby?!"

The trouble with Mr. Facebook was that he never seemed to be at my side to clean up my mess when I needed the help. I cursed myself and Mr. Facebook, as I looked down at the sweet and handsome man sleeping soundly in the silky sheets. Fretting that my Facebook friends, my boss, and especially my mother (who wasn't on Facebook at the time but had plenty of friends who were) would freak out if they heard I had a new life-changing status: married.

My new husband, Karl, awoke to the sound of my sobbing and asked me if I was crying because I regretted the marriage. "No, honey," I told him. "That is *not* the problem. Here's the deal, my mom is going to *kill* me. And if somebody posts our marriage photos on Facebook and my boss sees them, I'm so busted. Rain check on a honeymoon, I've got to hurry back to work and do damage control in DC."

Sometimes I wonder how I was able to muster the strength to endure the long plane rides and layovers home. After strapping in my seatbelt for the final connection and fighting the urge to skip the flight in order to retreat into Karl's loving arms, I tried flipping through a tabloid magazine to distract myself from obsessive thoughts over the fact that while my real life status went from "single" to "married" in just a few months, my Facebook status still read "single." And I told myself I wasn't going to update it for a myriad of reasons.

One, I haven't quit my job yet, though I plan on it, if my boss discovers I just married a man who lives on the other side of the country and on a day when I was supposed to be back at work, my ass will be on the chopping block. Two, my mom, standing behind her strict Catholic beliefs, will try to convince me to annul the wedding and I sure don't want my slippery relationship status to go from "married" to "divorced" in one week! Three, I don't want to hurt the feelings of close girlfriends with whom I haven't yet shared the news if they stumble upon an elopement post or photo before I have called them.

While heading home in a cab, I called three of my most trusted confidantes and pleaded with them to hurry over for some kind of a "Facebook Mission

Impossible" type-brainstorming meeting. Each of them answered my pleas to the same tune, "So that text you sent me in Vegas was really true? Are you shitting me?!," To which I replied, "Yes, I'm married!" Trish said, "I'll be there in five." John said, "We have to talk." And then, after not having returned several of my mother's voicemails she had left me while I was still in Vegas, I mustered up the courage to call her. As expected, my mom went completely ballistic when I told her the news of our elopement. A few profanities were shouted back at me into the receiver and then she hung up the phone.

The pep talk I had so yearned to have with my confidantes turned into a late night pity party. John said, as he took his last sip of wine, "Well...if it works out, it will be a great story. And if it doesn't, everyone will say I told you so." Then Trish and Holly chimed in, "You can always get an annulment." I didn't want my marriage annulled. I just wanted any potential Facebook postings that might leak to be annulled and I wanted some badly needed sleep so I kicked them out and tried to mentally prepare myself for the work day ahead.

Disheveled and with bags under my eyes when I got into the office the next morning, I noticed that some of my coworkers were looking at me oddly upon my return. *Do they think I look like I just partied too hard in Vegas? Or, do they think I look like a woman who had just spent a few sleepless nights celebrating her elopement or worse, do I look like a woman fretting over her shotgun wedding? Damn, there's only one person who will know: Holly.*

I marched down the hall and straight into my other best friend's office. "Okay, gossip girl, who did you tell?" I demanded as I closed her office door and pulled up a chair for an emotionally fueled interrogation. Her beautiful big blue eyes widened and her pupils grew even larger than I had ever seen them as she whispered, "Rach, I didn't tell anyone that you eloped. But, oh shit, what if they overheard me talking on the phone with you yesterday?"

I so regretted making that call to Holly while she was at the office. After I spilled the beans, she didn't talk, she started screaming into the receiver at me with joy. Exclaiming over and over again, "No way! YOU ARE PUNKING ME!!! YOU ARE PUNKING ME!"

"Well, if anyone asks you what I called you about, or why I missed work, just say nothing." Knees shaking, I tiptoed through the hall, locked my office door, and logged onto my Facebook account.

As I had expected, several of my friends had grown curious as to why my wall, which I usually updated hourly, had suddenly gone silent. My wall was filled with questions: "Well, what happened in Vegas?" and "Unlike you to not post pics of Sin City! Please share!" I wanted to post back "Please SHUT the F UP!" But I pushed on in search of any leaks within the walls of Facebook.

Determined to get my relationship back on track with Mr. Facebook and especially my increasingly suspicious friends, I typed names of friends into the search field of Facebook until my concentration was broken when my office phone rang, and I saw on the caller i.d. that it was my father and picked up the receiver. "Hey, Rah," he said. "I just wanted to let you know that you have a visitor coming." That could mean only one person, my mother. Uninvited, my mother had boarded a flight from Minneapolis to DC to intervene.

A full-on family emergency had been declared but rather than deal with it, I spent the rest of the day deleting curious questions and posts from my wall, including a growing number from colleagues who couldn't help but notice something brewing.

The next thing I knew, my unexpected mother was glaring at me from my office guest chair. I wished I could delete her incessant nagging and the "I didn't know your mom was coming to visit!" and "What's the occasion?" posts from already matrimonially suspicious co-workers.

Six days later, my mom finally gave up and left after many unsuccessful attempts to convince me and Karl, who had flown in and out of DC at the last minute for moral support, to file for an annulment. My father even flew in the weekend. Karl and I, in an attempt for us all to get along like civilized adults, took them to a fancy Italian restaurant for dinner that Saturday. Lets just say the evening did not go well. My mom leaned in to Karl as he took his first bite of a warm garlic roll and said "Do you know I am closer in age to you than you are to my daughter, Karl?"

Awkward.

Karl, being the soft spoken person he is, tried to be

conciliatory. "Yes, Sue. I was never married before. I got started late in life choosing to focus on my career."

Karl and I even went so far as to give up my bed for my parents to sleep in that evening to placate the tension. He slept on the living room floor. I slept on the couch. *Talk about awkward and uncomfortable.*

"Is he really putting up with all of this family drama for me?" I felt completely loved by him and completely estranged by my family, all at once.

Finally, Mom gave up and left. Karl returned to Denver. And I returned to my bed. I was still a new bride, but I was totally alone. Alone with my thoughts.

Yes, I thought, marriage is a major commitment. And, yes, family ties matter. I loved my mother, but I loved Karl, too. It hurt that instead of accepting my joy, Mom was judging it. Neither of us could convince the other to change. I felt like I was in a lose-lose situation: please my mother, but lose Karl; follow my heart's desire to be Karl's wife, but lose my family.

I called Karl in tears.

"Karl, thank you for being there," I sniffed.

"I love you, honey. You know that," he replied.

"I know. And I love you, too. I'm proud to be your wife. But—" "But what?"

"But I need to give some serious thought about what my mom said."

"Do you mean to say you're really seriously thinking about getting an annulment just to please your mom?" There was hurt in his voice. "If that is what you want to do, I will stand by you."

"No. It's not what I want."

"Rachel, I don't want to get an annulment either. I only want to do what makes you happy."

"I at least want to give some serious thought to what she said. She's my mother, Karl!" I sobbed.

Karl sighed and waited silently until my sobs calmed to just a few whimpers. Finally he spoke. "I love you, Rachel," he said gently. "I always will, even if it means you choose to walk away."

After our phone call, I poured a hot bath to unwind — and think. I brought up a large coffee mug filled with my favorite Columbian coffee from the drafty kitchen and rested it unsteadily on the tub's ledge while I stepped into the bath. The hot coffee nor the warm bath could quench the cold I felt in my soul.

As I sunk down into the sudsy water, I realized how much I craved acceptance. I felt Karl's confident and unconditional love. Even his family warmly welcomed me into theirs — once they got over their shock. But the pain of Mom's judgment and condemnation was excruciating. I desperately wanted my family to accept my decision to marry Karl.

Desperate. That's how I felt. Even though the claw foot tub was womblike, there was an emptiness within me.

I picked up my razor and slowly turned it over and over in my hand.

If I slit my wrists, I thought, I'll be able to make the pain go away. Forever.

I sat there for a long time, razor in my hand, having the most intense private conversation a person can ever have. A conversation about whether to live — or die.

Much of that conversation was a confused emotional jumble. I felt bad for dragging Karl into the drama with my family, but I also found myself thinking about my Facebook family and how I yearned for acceptance there, too. How would my Facebook friends react if I killed myself?

As shallow as this sounds, I realized I was still in love with the rush I got from my tumultuous affair with Mr. Facebook. I feared that if I quit on us, he'd simply move on as if I'd never existed. My Facebook "friends" would gossip about me and how I'd "failed" at life. I couldn't let that happen. I just couldn't.

I put down the razor, toweled off, plugged in my laptop and resumed my "Pollyanna postings."

To this day, I still can't comprehend how I had gotten to such a low point that murdering myself was a serious option. I was unable to come to honest terms with myself over the family drama and my need to be accepted. In a twisted way, my infatuation with Facebook saved my life.

I quickly grew exhausted from all the worry and the physical exertion I was putting into preventing this Facebook five alarm fire from spreading. My life would've been much easier had I just told my boss right away, but I was still unsure if I was planning on resigning in order to move to Colorado or if I was going to remain in DC. Plus, I was afraid if my boss thought what I did in Vegas was as foolish as my mom did, my story could affect my respectable standing at the firm.

With my new platinum wedding band tucked safely away in my pocket, I ran laps around the office monitoring the few coworkers who I believed were privy to my secret, thanks to my screaming banshee best friend. I spent the rest of my second work week as a married woman, using my un-billable office hours to pay office visits to suspicious coworkers in order to rebut the marriage rumors which were circulating on Facebook and in the office. As John Wayne once said, it was getting to be "ri-goddamn-diculous."

The Facebook fidelity fires finally died down at the close of June, and I confessed the "one day late back to work" story to my boss while handing in my resignation letter in order to be with my husband who was living 2,000 miles away. Luckily, even though the head honchos at the agency were a bit taken aback, they laughed when I showed them the John Wayne chapel wedding pictures and threw me a going away party.

I was grateful to be alive to celebrate my 33rd birthday and so relieved to see my new husband again who had flown in to help me pack. And I can't forget the icing on the cake; the abundance of goodbyes and happy birthday posts that populated my wall during my final week of living in DC. *I may have endured a hellish month of drama, but I'm so relieved that I didn't listen to the angel and quit Facebook. I will be more careful. Me and Mr. Facebook are gonna be A-Okay.*

Karl and I piled my belongings into a Penske truck and we headed cross-country to begin our new married life together in Denver. I told myself that with each passing mile I was leaving behind my Facebook preoccupation in order to embark on a fresh start where I would become Facebook footloose and fancy-free. While I would continue to use Facebook, I vowed to myself that it would be in small doses and completely drama-free. By only allowing myself a Facebook fix now and then, I hoped to make Denver my place to start a new chapter of married life versus my old online life. Little did I know how hard keeping my Facebook vows would be.

CHAPTER FIVE

Status: Rachel Ruff is "ga-ga" over her new Facebook friends

"Choose thy friends like thy books, few but choice."
—James Howell

On The mOrning Of augusT 3, 2008, the long cross-country journey to my new life while unattached to a USB umbilical cord was finally over. Karl and I finished unloading the moving truck of what little belongings I had salvaged by three o'clock that afternoon. Only my most sentimental possessions like my grandmother's china, some cherished gifts from other family members, high-end baking pans and utensils, and my most treasured and custom framed oil pieces, which I had painted in the years past, made the cut to my new life in Denver. I sold every piece of furniture on Craigslist after I learned the 47-year-old-bachelor-turned-husband of mine, whose apartment I had never visited prior to our marriage, was already stocked full of home accessories.

Feeling giddy with the excitement over our new life

together, we headed out on the town to grab a bite and meet up with Karl's local friends and a few of my old Marietta, Georgia high school friends who had relocated to Denver as well. Thanks to Facebook I had discovered them! Once again, weighing the cost benefit of being on vs. off of Facebook, Mr. Facebook won. Especially because I held the status of: "new girl in town."

At a local Mexican cantina, one of my friends toasted my arrival and announced to the table, "I'm going to create a "Denver Sunday fun-day" album!" I almost leapt over the mound of guacamole in front of me to kiss her, but I thought the more polite thing to do would be a toast. I clinked my fishbowl of a margarita glass to hers and exclaimed, "Wait till our old A-T-L classmates see us together in the Rockies now!" Thanks to my girlfriend and the photo album app I was freed of the task of "tagging" myself for my first Denver update and therefore was able to remain free from the distraction of Facebook for yet another 24 hours, thereby setting an all-time personal record: Six whole days of being off of Facebook due to the five days of drive time and the one day of unpacking. With all that time I was able to focus my energies on finding new cabinets for my possessions and adding a more feminine touch to the bachelor pad now turned love nest, or so I thought. My new life is exciting. *I'm busy and happy, I've got this balancing Facebook usage thing down.*

Talk about delusional. After three hours of swiftly unpacking boxes, shoving gold-plated flower patterned china in between my husband's piles of climbing rope and polo gear, I called out to Karl, "Finished unpacking, honey, I'm starving!" In the kitchen I discovered him busy setting up my Apple account on his laptop. I forgot all about my grumbling tummy.

Rather than lighting candles, making dinner preparations, or slipping into some sexy lingerie to turn Karl on, I scooted him from the keyboard in order to get fed by the Apple computer and turned on by Mr. Facebook via catching up on two-weeks worth of unopened Facebook messages I had been desperately waiting to dive in to. I hoped that no one had forgotten me. Right before Karl's eyes, his breakfast nook had morphed into his wife's new meeting place for her other man, Mr. Facebook. My husband's computer was about to become my portal to the world of Facebook because my laptop had been the property of the PR firm.

Later that week I caught up on the abundance of gleeful tidings that were still trickling in as well as the new posts below the tagged photos of us in the "Sunday Fun-day album." My fear that everyone had forgotten about me turned out to be a complete farce. *"Rach. You don't even look like the Rachel Ruff from high school! Denver rocks! You ready for visitors yet?!"* Inspired to wow them even more, I uploaded the evidence of our Vegas wedding in a Facebook album I created, titled "What happens in Vegas." I was especially eager to finally share the picture which I had only texted to a few of my best friends: The candid snapshot my husband had taken of me kissing a life-sized poster of

John Wayne just after we said our vows. Ironically, the same photo that had caused me such grief and night sweats about being Face-booked without my permission garnered the most thumbs ups of all the Facebook photos I had ever posted.

My third task, change my status from single to married. Step 4: Update my location to Denver, CO. I smiled proudly at my profile edits which had uploaded to the news feed in record speed, "Phew, no mean jabs or jokes aimed at my unexpected life-changing status so far."

To ring in our first full week together in Denver, Karl turned on a romantic Joni Mitchell album and the song "A Case of You" began playing as he uncorked a bottle of wine to toast our first stay-at-home Saturday date night. After clinking glasses with Karl, I took a sip of my wine and sat back down at the dining room table to pay attention to my other darling, Mr. Facebook.

As Joni's melancholically beautiful lyrics trailed on, ...*You're so bitter, bitter and so sweet,* I realized how absolutely in tune the words were with how I felt about my beloved Mr. Facebook.

And then I raised my glass to the computer screen glowing alongside the candelabras' last flickering wicks, as the showcased status updates shined on brightly, "Rachel Ruff is now married " and "Rachel Ruff now resides in Denver" while humming along in my best smoky-voiced, Joni Mitchell imitation, *"I could drink a case of you, I could drink a case of you."* My page was flooded with a gamut of goodwill comments. I couldn't believe that I had gained 100 more responses to my relocation and marital status updates compared to the 30 I had reaped on my birthday just the month before. I also scored an overwhelmingly colossal amount of thumbs up hits and a lot of jovial inquisitions too. The majority of my wall comments read:

"You kept your maiden name?"
"Who is the lucky man?"
"What is his name? I want to friend him on Facebook!"
"Is this a new guy, I thought you were already married?!"

But my wine-induced buzz had cloyingly crept up on me and began acting as a Facebook depressant. I sighed as I looked over at my frilly pink ceramic cake plate my mom had given me eight years before, which looked out of place in its new home, the sterile stainless steel kitchen decorated with only Ginza knives which screamed "A bachelor lives here!," and I thought of how my wall was full of friend comments, but bereft of any family members' postings to check in on me. I was still family-friendless on Facebook, and my newest kin, Karl, was nowhere to be found in our tiny apartment for consolation. *He must've slipped away to bed, to recuperate from the big move... I wish I could stop and recharge too but my mind can't stop obsessing over Facebook and the family.*

My wall was bereft of mommy postings like, "Honey, did you two make the trip safe?" or my only sibling asking, "How are the newlyweds? Do you like your new condo?" or "When can we come for a Broncos game? I hear fall in Colorado is beautiful." They still had not friend requested me nor had I asked them in return. I guess a part of me was relieved that I wouldn't have to worry about how they might judge my wall or post comments regarding our marriage. They didn't approve of our matrimony process, and I was pretty certain they wouldn't approve of my Facebook persona either.

When I finally crawled into bed at 3 a.m. next to my already peacefully sleeping spouse, a thick blanket of melancholy enveloped me. I thought back to earlier that summer, when my endearingly captivating and intoxicating elopement news had morphed into a miserable post-marriage mania vexed with threats of pious intervention from my mother and her accusations of insanity as my state of mind. Instead of counting sheep, I tallied up the screaming fights I had with her when she found out about my marriage.

Finally, exhaustion set in and I heaved a big, "Thank you, God, for giving me the strength to not go through with suicide over Facebook drama and annulling our marriage for the sake of pleasing others." And I cuddled up to Karl, the only love of my life bigger than Mr. Facebook.

As fall was approaching and the leaves were changing, my restless sleep status remained the same. Night after night, my sleep increasingly became interrupted with fits of tossing and turning from nightmares. I was reliving, in a sense, re-runs of those old Facebook fears. I kept envisioning a bunch of nasty messages from friends and family on my wall claiming I was foolish for eloping and I even dreamt that my old boss had posted "You are fired" on my wall for everyone to see. The most horrific part of those awful scenarios was how helpless and humiliated I felt in not being able to control what others were sharing about me on my wall. I was exhausted from running from the digital dream demons and not getting any peaceful shut eye. I would crawl out of bed and join my new husband in the kitchen while trying to conceal the anxiety I was feeling.

Usually, Karl had no idea how late I would stay awake tormenting myself with Facebook worries, nor did he have any idea that I had once considered killing myself over our post-Vegas drama. Until one morning when the puffy bags under my bloodshot eyes gave me away.

"What's a matter, honey? Do you miss your friends? You were up pretty late posting on your Facebook wall last night. What time did you go to bed?"

Sheepishly I replied, "I didn't, Karl." I was embarrassed about my admission because I worried he might think I had a Facebook addiction.

Do I? I wondered. *No, I am just lonely. I just got carried away with hitting the "refresh" button on my friends' intoxicating walls laced with their weekend partying updates.*

Marlene Dietrich once said, "It's the friends you can call up at four a.m. that matter." *Did the friends' Facebook walls I was pulling up at 4 a.m. matter that much to me in actuality?* I wondered. Why didn't I just call them up? Could I even call them up? No way. I didn't know if these friends were really true friends and I think I was afraid to find out. Instead I chose to fake my newfound love of Denver life with glamorous status updates.

Did my desire to convince everyone that I was the most popular girl in Denver backfire? Like an avalanche, my feelings of isolation in the new town of Denver, in which I was now unemployed and bereft of friends or family, quickly caught up with me, as if I were eating alone at one of the vacant tables in the high school cafeteria all over again. Other than a slew of friend requests, no one was asking me out to coffee.

I had reached an all time low in the mile-high city within less than two months of having moved there in August. Not even the mountainscape from our kitchen windows with its dance of bright gold Aspen leaves amid the first unexpected and early first week of October snowfall could cheer me. So I concocted a plan to cure my latest bout of digital depression. *I would have to convince Karl to join Facebook.*

"Karl, please, you *have* to get on Facebook for me because I don't think anyone believes you are real except for the three friends of mine who met you in DC. I miss the fact that my sister and mom will never be my friend on Facebook, or in my life. I miss my friends in DC."

"Baby doll, you know I don't do Facebook." I felt terribly deflated by his response. While he handed me a fresh cup of coffee, he cheerily bargained, "Hey, there's a party tonight I'll take you to. Making new friends in town will help you feel less lonely."

Humph. What a lame peace offering, I thought to myself and I put on my best "pouty face" imitation to let him know I was more than displeased with his compromise. He finally caved in. "Okay. Okay. I will give Facebook a try for you."

I went from feeling slapped down to experiencing an exuberance of complete jubilation within five seconds flat. I gave Karl a big kiss and ushered him into his office to hurry up and get himself signed up. Not only did I hope to score some more friends' approval over our unconventional marriage once Karl joined. I was relieved that they could get to know and friend him, and most importantly that I could prove to the doubters that he did exist. I would also gain the ability to fill a blank on my wall that I had never inserted before; the "Rachel Ruff is married to:_____" link. I was giddy with delight about the status link I would then be able to concoct. *"Rachel Ruff is married to: Karl Osterbuhr."*

My husband training is going well. I chuckled to myself, as I settled back down into the kitchen table's stiff chair in ready position in order to pounce on the new "Facebook friend request" as soon as it filtered in. I assumed my world would now be in perfect harmony as all of the posting planets were becoming aligned. *I so wanted to be loved by my Facebook world and I wanted my Facebook friends to love Karl as much as I did and I wanted Karl to love Facebook back! Amen!*

That was my silent prayer. Ten minutes later my petition was answered. I heard Karl's voice coming from the other room. Sounding like a little school boy who was letting his mom know that he had dutifully finished his homework, in a monotone voice he said, "I'm on Facebook, honey."

I excitedly typed *Karl Osterbuhr* into the Facebook search engine field which connected me to his new Facebook page, the page that I had sought in vain when we had just met. I clicked accept and he now had one friend: me! As soon as I inserted my married status update link on my wall steering everyone to Karl's page, he received a plethora of friend requests from my friends who were eagerly waiting for Karl to accept them so they could get a good look at him.

Much to their dismay, my handsome husband, being as private as he is, chose to use for his profile picture an image of his favorite athlete: a famous polo player mounted on a horse, swinging a mallet, but he had edited the head off of the rider.

Soon after he posted his profile image, I received a lot of snippy comments, "Why is your hubby hiding his face? What, is he not hot?!" I couldn't win. *Geez, I finally get Karl on Facebook, and now I have to fight to get the shy guy's face on? Ugh, I give up.*

I changed gears from reading my wall of "Is he hot?" inquisitions and moved on to planning a fun weekend itinerary for my first guest who was coming to Denver to visit me in five more days, my best friend Holly. *Finally, I am going to have a real friend to hit the town with me!* And I stepped away from Facebook to get busy tidying the guest room.

Karl had taken me out on the town all weekend and with each new introduction to the who's who of Denver, I began to realize that our elopement story, which had seemed preposterous to my parents, was a great conversation starter and evidence of my "coolness" to these new Denver people. Their eyes would widen in amazement as they raised their glasses to toast my good fortune. And my *coup de foudre* would follow when these new friends would ask me to friend them on Facebook. I would become more enamored with them when they would add snapshots of me to their Facebook photo albums, like the one of me sticking my head in a friend's oven while being pretend shoved onto an oven rack by another new friend. Being "tagged" at events and captured in their photos, no matter how uncouth, made me feel as if I were a proud accessory of their exciting lives; that I was included in their clique, and that I was truly accepted.

After I finished putting fresh sheets on the guest bed, I returned to the kitchen computer to bask in the glory of likes below my wall post: "Holly is coming to visit me! My first and best houseguest yet!" when an instant message from Lucia, a former employee of mine whom I hadn't talked to since leaving the PR firm, popped up on my screen.

The IM simply read, "Rachel, are you there?" to which I immediately wrote back, since I was happy in life and no longer in Facebook hiding, "Hi Lucia! How's it going?" My spirits had quickly lifted when I received Holly's travel news and I now felt I had exciting things to share once again.

With a quick turn around response of, "Not good." I hurriedly typed back, "What's wrong?!" She answered, "I'm trapped in Europe, my passport and my money were stolen." I thought it was strange she would reach out to me, as I knew she had a very close family and network of friends. So I simply put, "Call me." and provided my digits.

Five minutes later, after anxiously awaiting an IM to pop up or for the phone to ring, all I got in return was a cold IM reading, "Please just send me cash to this PO box." I was spooked as the response didn't sound like something sweet Lucia would post. This reply sounded like a scam. I immediately closed the IM box and logged off of Facebook. About an hour later, I visited her page to discover the real Lucia herself had typed in all caps, as her profile status: "DO NOT SEND MONEY TO THIS SCAM CLAIMING TO BE ME. SOMEONE HACKED INTO MY ACCOUNT."

When Holly arrived the next day, Lucia's scam was our hot topic of conversation, as Holly had been contacted by the fake Lucia as well. We decided to let Lucia's experience be a lesson in protecting our online security and reputation. I changed my password to an intricate jumble of letters and numbers in order to avoid becoming bait for any potential "Rachel-posing" hackers. We cruised in to Boulder for a shopping excursion one afternoon with Lady Gaga playing on the radio and witnessed yet another one of Denver's unforeseen yet not atypical snowstorms of the season begin to fall. We parked and began snapping photos of ourselves together in the snow and I excitedly shouted in a Valley girl accent, "Like OMG, Holly, this one is so totally going to be our new profile pic!" To which she replied to my half joking-half serious comment, "Me too, Rachie Poo!" Later that evening when we got back to the apartment, we uploaded our new profile pictures. Holly was someone whom I cherished both on-Facebook and off-Facebook. She was a rare specimen of my Facebook friends.

Basking in the joy of Holly's trip, my will to thrive in Denver and on Facebook was rejuvenated. As if my positive thoughts were being rewarded, I received several Halloween party RSVP emails the following week. I jumped for joy in my audience-less kitchen and shouted out to Karl who was working in his home office, "Baby! Can you 'fricking' believe that *five* different Facebook friends have extended invitations for us to attend their Halloween parties?"

He walked into the kitchen, and tenderly responded, "That's great honey. I knew you would make a lot of friends here" and leaned over my laptop to kiss me on the forehead. He was probably relieved to let go of his "Rachel's social committee chairman" role thanks to his new allegiance to Facebook.

I followed Holly's suggestion and dressed up as Lady Gaga for my new friends' Halloween gatherings. Of course, Mr. Facebook was whom I was *really* dressing up for. By mimicking Gaga's look, decked out in a zany and burlesque all black wardrobe with a sprinkle of risqué fishnets and cleavage, I figured I could really make my wall pop, or should I say, make my Facebook wall visitors' eyeballs pop when I uploaded the photos from the following night. I also symbolically chose to go as Gaga because I had always admired her unique ability to proudly exhibit whomever she wanted to be, whether or not others approved of her fashion statements and ideals.

That was the one thing I couldn't mimic. I wasn't yet tough enough to send friend requests to my family. Gaga calls her fans her "little monsters." I feared my family could potentially become my "big monsters" by haunting or harassing me on my wall.

By my first Halloween in Denver, I had acquired almost 100 new Facebook friends in just three weeks. On November 1, I had a grand total of almost 760 Facebook friends. "How had I ever gotten to the tipping point of deciding to kill myself as a way out of Facebook and family fears this summer? Did I forget the promise I had made to myself on the long haul to Denver? No. I will never allow gloom and digital doom to take the reins and steer my new life into digital damnation ever again," I pompously reminded myself.

Ironically, a week after Halloween, my first family member finally "friend requested" me. She was also the first person to comment below my freshly loaded "Halloween of 2008" photo album, below the photo of me wearing a black leotard, fishnet stockings and outrageously high stiletto boots while posing next to some new girlfriends. "Put some clothes on girl," she posted below the photo. I was mortified.

Her comment boomeranged me onto some of my high school friends' walls in the quest to compare what they had worn on Halloween. I wanted proof that my costume wasn't completely disgraceful and to reassure myself that my family was just a bunch of prudes. *Okay Seraphina was Lady Tarzan basically wearing only a washcloth and Jill went as a sexy Playboy bunny. Heck Seraphina is an elementary school teacher! I'm fine.*

Later that day, Holly chimed in below a Halloween pic I uploaded, "Lady RaRa, I wanna take a ride on your disco stick!" which is a lyric from GaGa's 2008 hit song, *Love Games*. Her sense of humor always made me bust out laughing. The tune was an inside joke between us about a guy she had once dated who had used the cheesy line on her. Trouble was, no one else knew that the comment she shared on my wall was about her, not *me*. Minutes after her posting, the comments and likes of my naughty picture came out of the woodwork, including "I have a disco stick you can ride" from a guy I hadn't seen since high school who never even gave me the time of day back then. I quickly deleted the comment, and while I was at it, expunged my relative's jab too.

A few days later, my social media mood pendulum had swung back to dismay over my low numbers in Halloween likes compared to some of my girlfriends I considered competition in the popularity on Facebook contest. A game in which they didn't even know they were competing. When suddenly "my woe-is-me" thinking was interrupted as Karl stormed out of his home office and into my Facebook opiate den, yelling, "Fuck Facebook. Get me off of this thing!"

Shocked, I said, "What happened?"

Pulling off his reading glasses, he bent down to look me straight in the eyes and said, "I am sick and tired of getting friend requests from people I don't even know or barely remember."

I desperately wanted to fire back, "Send them my way, the more the merrier" or "Okay but you are missing out!" Instead, out of respect for his private demeanor and because I kind of enjoyed the fact that his ex-girlfriend, whom he had friend request accepted against my wishes, would then be a non-issue, I dutifully stood by his desk and tried to walk him through the painstaking process of deactivating his account. But the deactivate settings looked tricky so I selfishly left him to figure out how to quit. After all, I had better things to do with my time, like upload the even racier "Lady RaRa" photos I had hesitated to share at first, but were now going up as my last ditch attempt to draw more attention to my Halloween album than my competition.

While I felt Karl's social media efforts stunk, his social outings strategy more than made up for it. After all, my husband, the full-blown introvert, was doing a pretty good job serving as my full-time personal Facebook photographer capturing me, the extrovert, out on the town. Thanks to him, I was quickly making new Facebook friends and getting great material to post on my wall. So I ceased pouting about Karl's rapid Facebook resignation, and got busy posting more shots of me crouching down on the bathroom floor, clad in my fishnet stockings, cleavage spilling over the black leotard's top, with my long hair tucked up under a platinum blonde bob wig and the one of me kissing Karl, who was dressed up as Brandon Lee in "The Crow."

Just a week later, like a department store manager trying to beat out its competition, I decided to early promote the upcoming ski season by posting on my wall a "How to make real snow cones" video link to my YouTube page. As I stood three feet deep in snow, with only my string bikini and white fury boots to keep me warm, I bent over scooping up the fresh powder while adding in "but make sure the snow is clean, NOT yellow!"

Who does that? Well, the real me to this day would still do that. But only in humor to share with a few of my best friends, my husband and his fun loving family. NOT 700 Facebook friends and 2,000 of the YouTube strangers who clicked on it. I had completely forgotten the consequences which followed my "What happens in Vegas" Facebook fiasco.

With each new tasteless photo I added, my little angel would whisper words of warning to me, over and over again.

Is the angel inferring that some of these "treats" might actually be disguised as "tricks?" After all, why did my new friend Doug post me in the T-shirt when I clearly didn't know the cold room temperature was making me "nipply?" I wouldn't have done that to him if he were in a similar, yet male-specific situation, like ball shrinkage.

But because I, who once felt like a corporate cadaver slowly dying at her K Street desk, now felt like a kid in a candy shop acquiring an endless supply of sweet friends to dump into my friend bucket, I continued to dismiss the fact that I was possibly setting my wall up to decay.

Case in point, on a November weekend getaway with Karl to New York City, a couple of handsome and slick-haired guys, unbeknownst to me, had snapped a photo of myself and two girls I met from Morocco while we were dancing atop a bar and kissing on each other. The morning after my tabletop three-some tango, I gasped when I checked in on Facebook. Posted front and center on my wall was a photo of us totally drunk-o dames wearing only miniskirts with an audience of male fans drooling up at us from the dance floor below. Now sober, the escapade captured on camera and on Facebook wasn't so funny to me anymore. To discover that my lascivious behavior had been captured and saved to Facebook by the "Italian stallions" as Karl and I had sarcastically nicknamed them, was humiliating.

Apparently, those New York hooligans must've remembered my name even though I sure do not remember accepting them as Facebook friends! How did this happen? I checked the Face-book timeline, which revealed that at exactly 12:57 a.m. I had actually accepted one guy's friend request. A "Rachel Ruff is now friends with Giovanni Mastretti" update was my evidence.

While Karl showered, I quickly deleted my tagged name from the photo hoping the stranger wouldn't re-tag me in the days to come. Trouble was, although I could remove my tagged name from the photo and the photo from my wall, I knew I would not be able to remove the photo from Facebook's existence itself.

Therefore, the guys' memories of me and their cheesy "Sexy hot messes dancing on a bar top" would live on, to my dismay.

Karl tried to coax me out of the hotel room for a few hours of brunch and sightseeing, but I was too busy monitoring these NYC punks' Facebook activity to make sure I wasn't re-tagged and to confirm that they hadn't snapped any other inappropriate photos of me. Karl finally gave up waiting on me, and muttered, "Facebook is nothing but drama." The door slammed hard behind him. Not bothering to look up from the laptop or chase him down, I went back to playing a stressful game of mouse-clicking between the two Italian stallions' walls. That's when someone else popped in. My online guardian angel. I had incorrectly assumed she had moved on to aid other social media souls tormented with digital drama. "Rachel, privacy rules do not apply in the vast social media cyber-sphere where Face-bookers with cell-phones equipped with cameras are lurking everywhere! You know better. How many times do I have to remind you of your Vegas experience? And exactly who do you think these New York Facebookers really want to be Facebook friends with? Your inner self? Or your mini-skirt? Have you invited social media vampires to suck the life out of you on your wall? Choosing to spend your New York trip visiting with Facebook rather than enjoying your time with Karl?"

I didn't welcome her uninvited interrogations. Instead, I barked back, "I'm not going to get ill from adding too many new friends. But I am sick and tired of you. I wish I could delete *you*." I was taking my anger out on her because I was upset that she was right. To entertain and to attract new friends, these were my Facebook priorities.

But I did shift gears and made it my mission to chase down Karl and apologize. Thankfully, I found my husband in Central Park and he quickly forgave me.

As we strolled hand in hand through the city's grand

park, he shook his head and with a confused expression on his face asked me, "What is it with your generation? Why do you all feel the need to share *everything* on Facebook and Tweeter?"

"Honey, it's Twitter."

While I could grammatically correct him, I couldn't answer his question with a logical response. Instead, I poked fun at our fifteen-year age difference by swinging his hand in mine and skipping along like a little kid as I chanted aloud, "Cuz, sharing is caring."

Until the devil interrupted our walk in the park to sarcastically address my worries just as I had mimicked Karl's concerns over my social media usage. "Gee. What more fun may lie in store for us within your Facebook funhouse of horror? How about a game of hide and seek with friends?"

I didn't like how the devil was taunting me and I began to realize that Karl might be right. *Perhaps some of the pics and comments I had posted could be considered over-sharing, not just to my relatives but to anyone who visited my Facebook page?* As I boarded our plane back to Denver at the end of the weekend, I felt a bead of sweat developing on my upper lip and wondered if I should delete all of the "racy" photos when we got home.

I had accumulated a plethora of profile pictures that might actually be considered soft porn to some of my friends but I guess I was going to have to learn the hard way how dangerous over-sharing could be because I was still in denial over my Facebook addiction.

Originally upset about the photo, I began to have a change of heart after they caused a positive domino effect. Mr. Mastretti's friends had begun flocking to my wall by the dozen after I accepted their requests to be my "friend" that weekend. With the increase in my friend list, a soured weekend was sweetened and I found another reason to accept the devil's rationalizations and continue to fight off my angel's urgent messages to quit. *Am I trying to mask my fears and insecurities by being an "open book" on Facebook? Isn't everyone over sharing?*

Thirty-thousand miles up in the clouds, the angel finally spat out an answer, "Not exactly, Miss Ruff... just you and your more popular Facebook friends, whom you so desperately want to be more 'thumbs upped' than and more 'liked' by."

As the plane made its rocky descent into Denver, I deemed the notion to deactivate my account to be completely preposterous but I promised myself that I would choose my postings and my "friends" more carefully from now on. The reason why I was compelled to over-share no longer continued to baffle me. I was starving for attention and acceptance and popularity.

Once again, a negative experience reminded me of how wrong I was in my thinking that I could escape from Facebook drama. While I admittedly agreed with the devil, more often times than my angel, during our euphemistic conversations on certain issues like the desire to increase my popularity, was I willing to continue on the quest for social media salvation? Which meant the risk of incurring hackers, fakers, liars, and stealers? Was I strong enough to accept the potential negative consequences?

Could I remain on Facebook without feeling like a rotted carcass being circled by vultures? Or should I cut off my ties with Facebook friends by killing off my Facebook account to be safe? At the time, those were my only two options and my "all or nothing" approach felt like a "lose-lose" situation.

CHAPTER SIX

Status: Rachel Ruff has been mass de-friended

*"Two or three things I know for sure,
and one of them is the way you can both hate and love
something you are not sure you understand."*
—Dorothy Allison

as The winTer hOlidays were fasT apprOaching, my husband's friend Tim introduced me to a friend of his, Renee. Upon meeting her, I felt uneasy with her demeanor, as she seemed a bit overbearing and brazen. But I sure wanted to be liked on Facebook by her and the "circle of cool chicks" to whom she claimed she could introduce me, so I accepted her friend request on Facebook.

Renee became clingy from the moment we met, calling me several times a day, constantly monitoring and posting on my Facebook page, and inviting herself to my get-togethers. She was constantly striving to convince me that everyone was jealous of her, that our mutual Facebook pals in Denver had discovered our close friendship via Facebook and were envious of our special bond. As a result, she claimed, they began "de-friending" her at a rapid rate. She said, "Who cares about them? They can go to hell. You are my new best friend anyway."

Gulp. I swallowed hard when she told me the news, as the feeling wasn't mutual. Robert Louis Stevenson once said, "A friend is a gift you give yourself." But what do you do if you want to return one?

Before I knew it, my sympathy for her overruled my instincts. After all, I knew the feeling of desperately wanting to make friends. Renee begged me to throw a New Year's Eve party and create an invite on Facebook but not send it to any of the girls who had de-friended her, so that she, "could finally have fun and not worry about the 'bitches' who were jealous of her in Denver."

I ponied up to her request and convinced Karl that we should host a party for all of my new friends who weren't *yet* anti-Renee to ring in 2009. I worked hard to make a festive Facebook email invitation promising a jolly good time and the majority of my local Facebook friends accepted, not only my offer to attend our party, but also Renee's Facebook friend request to be their friend. I was surprised when I saw their friend updates listing her name on their walls, because they hadn't even met her yet. I did not expect she would friend request them before the party, but sure enough she had. I soon discovered that she had sent each party invitee on our New Year's Eve guest list a personal message reading, "Rachel wants you and me to be Facebook friends."

Oh how sad, I thought. "Who does that?" I yelled to Karl as we tidied up our apartment and lit candles. He didn't even know who I was talking about, but he rightly assumed it had something to do with Facebook and mumbled his now-famous mantra, "Fuck Facebook drama."

But could I really fault Renee for trolling for my friends? After all, like me, she was suffering from a severe case of what psychologists call FOMO or Fear Of Missing Out, meaning "digitally generated, grass-is-greener thinking." She too, had a deep digital desire to showcase how spectacular her life was via her status updates, in order to assuage her social-life insecurities and alert her enemies she was "liked."

Throughout the New Year's Eve festivities, each time someone took a photo, Renee would trill, "Put it on Facebook!" Finally, I grew tired of her sophomoric antics while I was busy mingling with our guests, so I gave her my laptop and shared my Facebook account password with her so that she could upload the party pics to her little heart's desire while the rest of us counted down the minutes until midnight.

There Renee sat at the dining room table at my laptop with a big, goofy smile plastered on her face, her soft grey eyes glazed over with each new Facebook party update. Looking over at her, I realized that I must have appeared just as ridiculous to Karl when I had first logged onto Facebook, at that very same table, the day after I touched down in Denver.

In between taking bites of cake and big gulps of

champagne, Renee busily tagged and uploaded photos. And unbeknownst to me, as the 2009 ball dropped, I had let the ball drop on my Facebook account by sharing my Facebook password with her that evening.

At the end of the party, just as daylight was breaking, I showed guests downstairs to the front entrance where cabs waited in lines, while Karl took out the trash. When I arrived back upstairs, the only hot mess I saw still remaining, besides the strewn confetti and cake crumbs, was Renee. She was hurriedly wrapping her scarf and buttoning her ski coat as her eyes, now very bloodshot, darted nervously around our apartment. She seemed to want to get out of our place in a hurry.

"Renee, don't you think you should just spend the night?" I said. You've had too much to drink and there are a lot of drunk drivers out on the roads. Your car is safe parked in our lot. Call your mom and tell her you will be home in the morning."

After multiple, unsuccessful attempts to convince her to crash on our couch, out she went with a big canvas bag which I had originally assumed was her "sleep over" stash since she had crashed at our place before after having had one too many drinks. From the looks of her bag, though, the contents appeared to have doubled in size. But I was too tired to inquire. So I ushered her out the door and hit the hay.

After I awoke the next day at noon, exhausted from the previous night's festivities, before I even picked up the mop, I got busy working on my favorite chore; surveying my Facebook page. To my delight, as I reviewed the Facebook photos of the previous night's shenanigans that Renee and the others had shared on my wall, I felt warmed by the images exhibiting what a smashing good time we looked to have had.

At peace with the social media success my New Year's Eve party scored, I moved on to updating my status: "Amazing hubby is taking me out on a romantic dinner date to a fabulous 5-star restaurant tonight to celebrate our seven-month anniversary!," even though I was the one who pressured him into planning the date night.

I gloated over the fact that while everyone else was probably sprawled out on their couches, nursing their hangovers, I was about to have a second glamorous evening. After all, one must always make sure to boast to the best of 'em how good you got it, in order to assuage any Facebook FOMO concerns one may harbor about one's self. Someone truly should have posted, "Gag me with a spoon, Ruff" after I updated my wall with the celebratory fun that was about to be had by me and the hubby. But then again, would that have stopped my Facebook bragging? Nah.

Four hours later, while rushing to get ready for date night, I went into panic mode. I was madly leafing through my usually immaculate and color coordinated closet to discover a surplus of empty closet hangers. My nicest silk Prada dress was missing. So was another dress. I finally pulled down a pair of designer black skinny jeans to wear. "Was I losing my mind?" I wondered. "How could all of these items be misplaced in our tiny apartment loft?"

Though reeling with anger and confusion, I firmly instructed my impulsive, emotional self to chill out and pull it together for our anniversary date night. My angel quietly reminded me I could always "take action and inquire about the missing items on Facebook in the morning." It took all of my willpower to keep from posting, "My most prized possessions have gone missing from my bedroom!" that night. The struggle I had to put into placating my urge to share the drama on Facebook felt as I imagined a drug addict would feel trying to fight the impulse to inject a needle of heroin. But the angel in me convinced myself that checking in with my other boyfriend would ruin the intimate dinner Karl had planned for us.

The next morning, I filed a police report and then I gingerly called each of the partygoers who were in our place for the New Year's Eve party, asking each of them if they had, by chance, "borrowed" any of my things and forgotten to tell me. Every one of them seemed a bit taken aback. However, one partygoer recalled the only person who was out of sight while we all went downstairs to say our good-byes was Renee. The only attendee I had not yet called. Perhaps because I already was subconsciously aware that she might be the perpetrator.

Karl's friend even went so far as to share her own personal angst about Renee with me, "Rach, she is bad news. I didn't want to tell you because you are new to town, but she has an old roommate, Carly, who claims to have had the exact same thing happen to her."

"What?! You mean she stole from her closet, and

her jewelry and makeup drawers too?" "You should just call her," Karl's friend said. She then gave me the woman's number before promptly hanging up.

Desperation set in the next morning as I stared down at the sticky note where I had scribbled the roommate's digits. After I hesitatingly shared my suspicions about Renee, Carly reassured me and listed a myriad of her own missing items that she believed Renee had stolen, including a bicycle, some of her favorite designer jeans, her makeup, and even some of her sexy lingerie. Carly went on to suggest that I do as she had done, and de-friend Renee on Facebook.

Carly then offered her sympathy and encouraged me to keep watch, via my Facebook friends, to see if any of my clothes or jewelry were spotted on Renee, who she dubbed the "single white female" of Denver. While I still felt betrayed, I appreciated Carly's Facebook detective strategy.

Less than hour after our phone conversation, Carly sent me a Facebook friend request, which I accepted. The Facebook update, "Rachel is now friends with Carly" that popped up on my wall must have served as a red flag for Renee. I received one irate call after another from Renee that afternoon, all of which I let go straight into voicemail. "How are you friends with Carly? Don't you know she is the one I told you about who stole all my stuff? She is a BITCH!" When I listened to her messages, I heard anger in Renee's voice but I also thought I heard panic and guilt in her tone.

There was no way in hell I was about discuss the disappearance of my $5,000 dollars worth of sentimental valuables with her. But unlike Carly, I decided not to de-friend Renee. My mantra became "Keep your Facebook friends close and your enemies even closer." I guess Renee had the same idea, as she was constantly monitoring my Facebook page and continuing to call me several times a day to see if I had made any discoveries in who had stolen my things. She had even gone so far as to provide me with names of resale stores and pawn shops around town to check on my missing items. I played clueless about my suspicions about her, even calling every used clothing and jewelry vendor to which she referred me.

Though I had filed a police report and noted my suspicions that morning, the cops said I had to have concrete evidence the items were stolen.

Frustrated by the politics required to elicit a detective's participation in locating my "missing items," as they coined them, I briefly put my Facebook investigation aside to look for concrete evidence. First stop, Denver County's online public police records. To my disgust, below Renee's name was a shoplifting report with a major department store listed as the plaintiff.

Furious about the discovery, but also a bit more motivated to get back to my Facebook investigation, I messaged a few more of her former Facebook friends, as well as some of her current Facebook friends, whom my new "friend" Carly had referred me to and inquired whether they had experienced anything like I had. I received several emails back from these local Facebookers, each one claiming possessions gone missing after she had visited their homes, a watch, a camera, etc.

One Facebook friend of Renee's went so far as to tell me that she thought she saw her in my Prada dress, Tiffany sunglasses and Dolce & Gabbana scarf at an event the weekend before. She proceeded to describe, spot on; my missing gold-plated sunglasses, the silver hoop earrings and the silk polka dot dress with an intricate lace pattern. "Go look on Renee's photo album from the event. See if they're yours." Had Facebook evidence been right under my nose in one of her photo albums? But where were my most prized shoes, my wedding gift from Karl?

I quickly typed in Renee's name to get to her page but discovered I could no longer find her on Facebook. The screen simply read: *"The page you requested was not found. You may have clicked an expired link or mistyped the address. Some web addresses are case sensitive. Return home. Go back to the previous page."*

Had this feisty redheaded "single white female" beaten me to the punch? *She not only had de-friended me but she must have gone into her privacy settings and blocked me!* To make doubly sure she hadn't "quit" Facebook but actually de-friended and blocked me, the mutual pal who saw her wearing my missing items, came over and pulled up her Facebook account to show me that Renee's profile wall was still active.

The wild goose chase was finally over the next evening. My mole, another mutual girlfriend, bravely volunteered to set up a girl's night out with her, and looked through her closet that night while Renee was putting on make-up in the bathroom. She retrieved a pair of my $680.00 gold embossed leather stilettos hidden beneath a pile of jeans, which she stuffed in her duffel bag and delivered to me the next morning.

I hugged and kissed her. I was so grateful for her great detective work. Next I showed her how my Facebook friend list had sharply declined by twenty of my local friends overnight. "I really don't consider these club hoppers to be my friends, as I just recently met them out with Renee, I am really confused."

My mole pulled up a chair and said, "Rach, she is on a mission to get, as she calls it, 'revenge on Ruff.' Dimitri told me that she has been sending email requests to have you mass-defriended."

"Oh my God, he was one of them who de-friended me! First, she preys upon my closet? And now my Facebook friends?" I was so angry I was shaking.

How ironic. I thought to myself. *I am about to ignite a Facebook five-alarm fire once again, but this time I don't have a husband to conceal, but a thief to reveal.* "This is now Facebook war," I told my friend.

Immediately after showing her out of the apartment, I took a sexy photo of my freshly manicured toes peeking out of my stolen shoes, uploaded it to my Facebook page and a posted a caption below that read: *"Home sweet home."*

Fighting the urge to share where the shoes were found, but giving in to my anger fueled impulse, I added another comment to my wall, "Karma is a bitch."

Within minutes of my posting, I had garnered almost 50 responses from friends who were in the know about my stolen items. And then the phone rang. My mole yelled back into the receiver, "DO NOT send any more emails to me about Renee, or anyone for that matter. She just called me and went ballistic screaming that she knew I was the actual one who stole your shoes. She is crazy. She is using me as the scapegoat."

"What?"

"She sounded really wasted and drunkenly boasted of how she had stolen your Facebook password when she was over and how she used it to delete your friends on Facebook. And get this; Renee had intercepted email messages from the friend who thought she saw her in your dress and other accessories. Your personal email account password was the same as your Facebook one I am guessing?! Since you blocked her from your Facebook wall she told me she logged into your account and saw the shoe picture you posted which she will probably delete from your wall unless you hurry up and change your password. She is going to kill us. I'm seriously freaked out."

I couldn't believe what I was hearing. I quickly hung up, went into Facebook's security settings, and changed my password. Here I was thinking people had de-friended me, while they assumed I had de-friended them. "No wonder when I would call and ask Dimitri and the others to meet me out for a cocktail in the name of damage control, they would shun me," I told Karl, who had heard the clamor and walked into the kitchen looking more amused than sympathetic, as if he thought this escapade would finally convert his besotted wife into his "Fuck Facebook" club.

Then the phone rang again and the call was from another concerned Facebook friend who told me that Renee had just sent a group Facebook email alerting friends, including important potential business contacts with whom I was trying to network, that "The new girl in town, Rachel Ruff, is a lying, stealing bitch. Please delete her from your friend list for your own good." Her "de-friend Rachel Ruff" worked, as another ten people went missing from my Facebook friend list. She was on a mission to defame me.

The sudden decline of my Facebook friends, due to the fact that this woman had hacked into my Facebook profile, using the password which I stupidly shared with her at the party, made me angry. So I quickly concocted a strategy to repair my Facebook reputation. Rather than defaming her name, as she had done mine, I decided to play hardball. I called the detective on the case and turned Renee in. The detective told me I needed evidence to charge Renee. Once I told her about the shoe retrieval from Renee's closet, she interviewed my "mole" for further testimony and then put out a warrant for Renee.

The next day, after she was officially charged with theft, I captured a screen grab from the Denver County records listing both her shoplifting theft and the new one with my name as plaintiff. "Now," I snickered, as I recklessly posted the public link onto my profile page, "the drama is over." But it wasn't. A few hours later the screen grab went missing, as well as the trail of my friend's 50 plus "OMG!!!" comments. "But how could that be?" I wondered. "No one has the power to remove postings from my wall but me. She doesn't have my password anymore."

The morning after, the mystery was solved. Renee wasn't the culprit. Facebook sent me an email stating they were informing me of my "misuse" and had removed the "offensive" posting from my wall and not to post libel again or "I would lose Facebook privileges," as in, next time, they would shut down my account. Sadly, my ego and my digital devil got the best of me as I had stooped to Renee's level. Even though the police report was a public record, I had to adhere to Facebook's moral standards, because it was a privately owned company, regardless of how immoral I felt Renee had been in stealing from a "friend."

I never did retrieve all of my stolen items and in my opinion, Renee never received the appropriate legal punishment. She was ordered to serve a few months of community service.

My unsuccessful attempt to use Facebook to expose the hard truths that exist beneath the facade of Facebook walls had backfired on me.

Though I wasn't the thief, I felt just as much of a villain as I had stooped to a level of social media psychosis by trying to prove to others that I was neither a "bitch" nor a "liar," as Renee claimed. Why did I feel the need to play out my detective drama all over Facebook? Why did I feel the need to prove myself to acquaintances who dropped me from their friend list? Did I miss them on my wall? They weren't even my *real* friends.

The extreme lengths I went to add strangers to my wall came with a high cost: 1) My online reputation with the Facebook team who sent me an email threatening to shut down my account for "misusing my wall." 2) My friendship with local Facebook-ers who had de-friended me. 3) My digital dignity.

While I felt resourceful in using Facebook as a detective tool, I had gone too far in broadcasting the outcome. My Facebook wall had come crashing down on me all over again. The consequences I faced after accepting a person whom I would have never "friended" in real life, had my life not revolved around Facebook, reinforced how badly I was behaving in order to grow my fan club, because that's really what I was longing for, fans *not* friends. And I felt humiliated by the fact that Mr. Facebook's team had threatened to shut my wall down as a punishment for my inappropriate posting behavior.

As a result, I finally acknowledged that I had never escaped my addiction to playing in my Facebook house of horrors, in which I kept blindly falling through friends' trap doors. No more would I allow strangers on my wall, I decided. But I wouldn't have to. Soon enough, some very familiar faces came knocking.

CHAPTER SEVEN

Status: Rachel Ruff is now friends with "Fam-damn-ily"

"You cannot say 'no' to the people you love, not often.
That's the secret. And then when you do, it has to sound
like a 'yes'. Or you have to make them say 'no.'
You have to take time and trouble."
—Mario Puzo, The Godfather

Even afTer The case was clOsed, I was still feeling ashamed over how I had handled the Renee robbery. Renee was one of those "social media skeletons" the angel had warned me about welcoming onto my wall. I was not proud of the shallow goose chase that I had launched on Facebook in my desperate attempts to get my belongings back. As a result, my passion for Mr. Facebook had temporarily waned yet again.

I could no longer hide the truth from myself and complacently remain social media stubborn. Just as the devil predicted back in New York, "How about a game of hide and seek with your friends in your Facebook funhouse of horror?," I went into hiding.

For the first time, I thought seriously about quitting Facebook. I would suppress my Facebook usage for a few days, like a smoker attempting to quit. Sometimes I would successfully coast along without taking a digital drag, other times I would become so desperate for approval that I would pick right back up and get almost physically nauseous from chain-posting.

I would receive a ping asking me to "live chat" when an old friend saw I was online and I would hide, choosing not respond. I'd simply "X" out of their invitation, and log out of my account. I didn't want to chat because I had started to feel that I didn't have anything good or authentic to chat about. In real life I was lonely, de-friended, and bored in Denver. I felt like I would let my Facebook persona and all of my Facebook friends down if I shared the true sadness I was harboring within. I believed that they depended on me for my Pollyanna postings rather than a real life update.

Almost as if Karl could sense I needed some R&R time to escape my unhappiness, he surprised me by booking us a belated honeymoon getaway to Mexico for a week in early February of 2009. *An escape from the social media storm I brewed?!? This could be the perfect remedy.* I worried that that I might slip up and post during our vacation, but my concerns were for naught. When we arrived at the resort I learned the Internet was not easily accessible so my Facebook hiatus was happening, like it or not.

But I sure as heck didn't give myself a Facebook break "from thinking about what to post when I got home," nor did I permit Karl a photography Facebook break. I quickly reverted to my old bad behavior after I realized I would now have something to show off. *Fucking brilliant! I can collect some exciting tales to post when I return! Now the cool kids will be able to see my jet set lifestyle!*

The professional camera he had brought along to shoot photos of exotic birds and architecture for his photography hobby, was re-assigned by me, his Facebook-posting-starved wife, to capture my every move so I could plaster the experiences on my Facebook page when we got home. I even took notes in my journal on ideal tags I would like to post to the pictures so I wouldn't forget. Here are a few samples from my Facebook journal I brought along to Mexico:

A "fish bowl" of a margarita aside a plate of homemade tortillas & holy guacamole!

This bird is trying to eat my cake! He's my new Facebook friend!

My fav watermelon bikini

Me & the executive chef [who I pulled out of the kitchen]

I love the bubbly! [Bubble bath and a bottle of Veuve Clicquot on a candlelit counter]

My swan [Heap of plush white towels the maid had arranged to look like a swan]

Homemade chocolate truffles at bedtime! [Which sat atop plush pillows on our silky bed]

This honeymoon suite is sweet! [About whales leaping from the water in the background as seen from our master bedroom's balcony vista]

While I scribbled madly in my journal, poor Karl obediently shot more and more photos of me, me, me, and me in my goddamn bikinis. *Barf. I'd be sick of looking at me if I were my friend on Facebook.*

On day three at the resort, Karl put his foot *and* his camera down. I was modeling one of my favorite poolside sundresses with a beautiful hibiscus lined pathway as my backdrop. I was barking orders at how to better frame me for the "perfect profile picture" when my photographer put the lens cap on and insisted we break to have a Mai-Tai and watch the sunset in peace and quiet by the pool. To my dismay, Karl then said, "I'm going to go put the camera in the room. Go get us a table."

About ten minutes later, he sat down at our table overlooking the bright orange sun which looked like it was going to plop from the sky and be swallowed by the sea at any second. We sat in awkward silence, not even commenting to each other on the breathtaking view. The server finally arrived and handed us our drinks. Not even pausing to make a toast, as was customary for him, Karl pulled out his cocktail straw, flicked it down onto the patio table, and took a big gulp. I was perplexed. I looked at him with a puzzled expression as I tried to peer through his dark sunglasses to get a read on him.

He finally grumbled, "Karl don't do straws."

Trying to break the ice, I cheerily answered back, "Well Rachel loves straws!"

"I know. You love straws and you love Facebook."

Ouch. I guess I had pushed my photographer's Facebook

button too far this time. Selfishly, instead of apologizing for my obnoxious behavior, I mentally tallied up if I had enough material to bring back with me to post to Facebook. I figured I did. "Give the guy a rest, Rachel." my angel counseled. "Do you want your husband to de-friend you because of your addiction?" She was right. I vowed I would never ask him to snap another photo on that trip in the name of Mr. Facebook. During our last two vacation days my attention was 100% geared towards spending time with my husband and we both really enjoyed the one-on-one time with no Internet distractions, no Facebook feuding. As we were checking out on our final afternoon, he sweetly looked over at me and said, "Stand over there honey. This will make a great closing shot for your Facebook photo album."

I smiled big and thought to myself, *Wow, even though I love Mr. Facebook a little too much, Karl's still willing to share me with him.*

Before I even unpacked the bags from our trip, I downloaded the photos from his camera, in between potty breaks that is, thanks to us contracting Montezuma's revenge, also known as traveler's diarrhea, (which of course, I shared with my friends on Facebook!). As I put together my *"Honeymoon at last"* photo album, I got a sinking feeling in my stomach, and it wasn't from the parasites. It was because my mom had finally come a-knocking on my wall.

My mother, whom I was estranged, since marrying Karl eight months before, had sent a friend request to me. I didn't know what to make of it. *Had she really asked me to friend her?* I already had enough peer pressure issues from Facebook. The last thing I needed was parental pressure. With each alert of her "pending friend request" reminder, I groused over what to do. To accept or not to accept? Can you really say no to an estranged family member who sends you a Facebook friend request?

My timid mom had joined the social utility site just a year after I (according to her) "made the mistake of eloping with Karl after three dates. The utter shock of your marriage gave me shingles and caused my eyebrows to fall out." Since that joyous day for Karl and me, which was the "most terrible week of her life," we had not spoken much.

The rift had driven us deeply into the mother-daughter doldrums and we have remained there ever since. But eight months after my marriage, still not on amicable terms, she wanted to "friend" me? I was confused. By accepting her as a Facebook friend, though she didn't accept my life choices, would I be relenting and perhaps even passively be accepting her judgment?

Did my mom think that by becoming my friend on Facebook she would awake one morning to a miraculous posting on her wall from me, her "prodigal daughter?" Something to the tune of, "Hey Mommy! So sorry I hurt you. Let me annul this wedding as you insisted and do it the 'right way' for you and the Catholic Church!"

She was, and actually still is, waiting for an apology from me for our "sudden wedding" and for "ruining your sister's birthday." Five years later, my husband and I are even more unapologetic. The only "sorry" we feel is over the fact that she has chosen not to partake in our joy. Our marital decision, unlike my fervent and frequently foolish Facebook postings, while impulsive, was neither wrong nor idiotic, but intuitive.

As the parental paranoia raced through my head, I wondered, *"Does she just want me to friend her in order to prove to her 'chatty Cathy' friends that all is peachy between us?"* I envisioned her wall: *Status update: Rachel is now friends with her mommy. Or would she put up a nice Facebook profile picture of her shingles and snap back at me publicly?*

You would think I was agonizing over how to placate an important and edgy business client with the effort I put into deciding whether or not to "accept" my mom. I fretted over which Facebook photos I should trash and which status updates I should delete if she were to have access to my page. I would also have to think of new and sweeter postings to put on my wall to impress my mom if I accepted her. Heck, dealing with all of those DC drama-filled clients seemed like a piece of cake compared to my dilly-dallying with family matters on Facebook.

I wondered if I was really strong enough to handle my mother snooping on all of my business via Facebook, when she wouldn't even speak to me on the phone. Finally I justified adding my mom because it would fatten my friend list and a little part of me wanted her to see how happy I was with Karl, especially after I had just posted our honeymoon photo album.

Here I was, a thirty-something woman, struggling to unfasten her mother's apron strings, yet still tied up in concealing her Facebook-isms from her mom. I checked and then double-checked the photos that seemed delete-able or block-worthy. Once my walls were completely bowdlerized of any Facebook filth, I dutifully accepted my mom. What a mistake.

After I friended my mother, "never write anything you wouldn't want your mother to see" began to serve as my new moral code for Facebook postings. On the bright side, I figured Mom might come in handy as a sort of virtual policewoman. Perhaps by having her as my friend I would become a more virtuous social sharer. The acronym PMS now took on a new meaning: *Postings Mommy Sound.* I was gonna play it safe.

However, by friending my mom I had opened the family floodgates. I began to receive an influx of friend requests from relatives. The only family member who didn't friend request me was my sister and that irked me and opened up a whole new can of Facebook worms.

Why doesn't my sister ask me to be a friend on Facebook now that my mom has? Doesn't she want me to see a glimpse of her life through her Facebook wall even though we still don't talk? If mom is my "friend" again, why can't she be my "friend" too?

Ironically, all of that worry over my mom Facebook bombing my wall was for naught. She rarely posted anything to my wall except information about a charity walk for the Polycystic Kidney Disease Foundation or a book signing event she was hosting for her memoir, *The Reluctant Donor.*

While I was not pleased with the strain in our mother/daughter relationship, I was very proud of Mother's selfless dedication to finding a cure for Polycystic Kidney Disease (PKD), as well as her heroic donation of her own kidney to save her sister's life, which Mom recounts in her nonfiction to help draw attention to the PKD disease and bring awareness about the need for more organ donors. I was more than happy to use my heavily trafficked wall as a vehicle for drawing attention to our family's cause.

As the daylight hours began to grow longer that spring, so did the time I spent in my bathrobe staring at Facebook. I went into full-time-Fear-Of-Missing-Out (FOMO) mode, becoming preoccupied with reviewing my friends' updates and accumulating almost two-hundred more friends. I should have been ecstatic about it, but I wasn't. I began to wonder if the saying, "the more money you have, the more unhappy you are" applies to the amount of Facebook friends one has as well.

From wall to wall I skulked, analyzing, criticizing, and obsessing over my friends' cheery and ambitious updates. And even more often, I scanned my mother's wall, hoping to get a glimpse into my estranged sister's life. *While we may not be Facebook friends, she is the only sister I have and I love her and miss her,* I thought to myself. Yet I would scowl when I detected that she was writing more on my mom's wall than I was. Out of sisterly jealousy, I feared she'd prove to be the better Facebook daughter.

One night, completely exhausted by my feelings of loneliness and envy, I drunk-Facebook posted, "I'm a bad banana with a greasy black peel." My Grinch status update didn't achieve much. In fact, no one even responded.

I soon found myself posting more frequent alcohol-fueled messages which gained notice, just not the notice I wanted. When "morning after" Facebook email alerts arrived with multiple subject lines reading "Someone has commented on your wall post," I would become bewildered and even frightened. "Huh? What wall post? I don't remember posting this picture of me holding a black baby doll last night?! Oh shit. OMG...No, did I write *that* below?!"

"Rachel Ruff just gave birth to a black baby." Oh yes, I had. I then proceeded to hit DELETE as quickly as I could on the erratic entry on which friends had commented, "Was the new mommy Drunk-booking last night? LOL!" I sure didn't want my mommy to see them. Nor anyone else for that matter.

Some drunk posts, such as "I'm flying out to visit my DC peeps this week!" were downright lies. After all, I couldn't afford to visit them, we had just spent too much on our Mexico vacation and I was still jobless. *Why in the hell did I post that?* I asked myself as I hit delete and removed their excited, "When are you arriving!?" "Can I pick you up at the airport?" comments.

I was still lying to bolster my Facebook reputation. The fibs were fueled by my feelings of missing out on the good times with real friends back in DC.

Living 3,000 miles away, I was afraid they were going to forget me unless I gave them the sense I would be visiting soon. So much for my Mexico retreat. What I truly needed to do was go on a complete exile from Facebook. But I didn't have a shepherd to show me the way out. Just a pesky angel, which I now realize was my conscience; my inner voice.

You don't know how someone is truly feeling simply by reading their postings, Rachel. Their heart may be expressing pain, loneliness, or frustration, just like you are hiding from your friends and family. Continuing to live in complete denial no matter how cheery your wall posts may appear to others is not a solution. Reach out to people in real life not just on Facebook. Quit hiding out.

Eschewing my own moral compass, I madly continued to check my wall and my friends' walls only to discover more uncensored digital doozies I had written at two in the morning while smashed, such as "Rachel Ruff is crushing up filberts." My unconscious actions were making me crazy. *If I were reading this post, I'm not even sure if I would believe it. If I was reading this as a friend, I would think about posting below, "Speaking of filberts Rachel, YOU are nuts."*

To impress upon my friends that I was not insane, which the drunk posts might have insinuated, I would soberly switch back to my tactic of cheerily posting "little nothings" the mornings after, such as "It's a beautiful day in the neighborhood, won't you be my neighbor?" I was trying to play the Mr. Rogers of Facebook, while inside I was more like Oscar the Grouch. Drinking was becoming a part of my problem, spinning me into a caustic cycle. *Big sip, bitter post, big sip, bitter post.*

No matter how much I tried to fill my Facebook wall with overly exaggerated and bubbly status updates, I was still seething that my friends' Facebook walls appeared to be glasses half full, while I continually viewed mine as half empty. I was very happily in love with Karl, but I began to realize that Mr. Facebook wasn't at my side "for better or for worse" like Karl always was. Mr. Facebook seemed to go M.I.A at the first sign I needed his support.

When I got home refreshed from a yoga class one May morning, I firmly swore to myself that rather than continue to hit the bottle and the "upload" button with drunken posts, I had to stop the vicious cycle. I decided that I'd try to focus instead on rekindling my culinary career. Scoring a steady paycheck rather than sporadic thumbs ups, I figured I would gain a much healthier outlook on life. I would switch my focus in life from playing house and perfecting my Facebook wall witticisms to improving my culinary skills, which was especially trying considering the somewhat complicated high-altitude baking issues of the mile-high city. As elevation rises, air pressure falls, which means that bakers living at 5280 feet may face fallen cakes or evaporation making the finished product taste dry. Another challenge stems from a lower boiling point, causing foods cooked in steam or boiling liquids to take longer to cook.

Let's flashback for a moment here. In the fall of 2000, I had briefly left my job as a CNN medical news producer in order to pursue a Pastry Arts culinary degree at L'Academie de Cuisine in Maryland. Basically, I went from being a news nerd to a muffin maker. Not the typical career path for a news producer.

But I wasn't just any baker, I graduated with honors and was hired to apprentice under President Reagan's former White House pastry chefs. Dozens of cream puffs later, barely a year out of school, I grew tired of the culinary clamor and desperately craved the noisy newsroom atmosphere. I returned to CNN, where I was tasked with serving as Dr. Sanjay Gupta's producer.

Fast forward to Denver, where I picked up my culinary tools and started getting catering gigs around the city. Meanwhile, I had finally accomplished my dream of having a thousand Facebook friends. Accumulating those numbers was exactly what kept me hanging on by a thread to my wall. Old friends began posting, "No wonder you never call me! You're just too busy on Facebook, you little social media diva." And "I love looking at your 'culinary creations' photo album! How impressive!"

One beautiful spring morning, I carefully dropped spoonfuls of cookie dough I had made for the mayor's press meeting onto a baking sheet. While I waited for the puff pastry to leaven, the oven timer to buzz, and the chocolates to melt, I used my catering downtime time to check in on Facebook.

During my sixth batch of cookies, I stepped away from the oven so that I could see if anyone had yet to thumbs up my status: "Rachel is baking chocolate chippers for the mayor right now." In just five minutes, I discovered that I had already scored a handful of likes and a few admiring comments.

Before long, I was so engaged in counting the likes and responding to the compliments that I failed to notice the acrid smell of burning cookies in the oven. That is, until the kitchen fire alarm began blaring. What had felt like seconds on Facebook during my pastry break must have been much longer.

Of course, I didn't stop to re-update my status and let everyone know of my Facebook induced gaffe: "Rachel Ruff just burnt her cookies from looking at her status for too long." That would be too uncool, too real. I'd rather burn my cookies than sear my culinary reputation online. Instead I used my precious time and ingredients to remake another batch of gourmet cookies, all because I forgot to set the timer. I was more loyal to Mr. Facebook than to Mr. Mayor.

Many Facebook users have discovered how distracting the site can be, but few have suffered consequences as severe as a woman I read about after I charred my cookies. In the spring of 2010, a woman made national news after she was arrested on charges of child neglect. According to media reports, her baby had died by drowning in the bathtub. The mother claimed that she had stepped away from the bathroom, for just a moment, to check on her Facebook alerts.

After reading about this woman, my angel chimed in, "How many years are you willing to spend locked up in a cell, i.e...on your computer?" She was right. Basically, that's exactly what I was doing. I hadn't killed anyone from my ungodly hours on Facebook but myself. The devil quickly interjected, "Facebook isn't killing your soul, Rach. Mr. Facebook loves you. Look at all these cookie comments!"

Most ovens are built with a timer to set and signal the user when the cooking process is done. On Facebook, as well as on many other interactive sites, one can easily whittle away hours without registering how long one has over-saturated oneself online. Social networking sites purposely do not have timers for users to set. In fact, the more people marinate in websites' page content, the more "dough" the sites make via advertising dollars.

According to a CNN.com article, "How much do Google, Facebook profit from your data?" all the great stuff we get for free from the Internet like the searches, the games, even Facebook, isn't really free. It's an exchange where companies are able to take user data, sell it to advertisers, and make money that allows them to give themselves a paycheck while keeping you afloat in free digital services.

But I hadn't completely learned my lesson about online privacy issues because a few days later, I was scammed by an email directing me to click on a link and type in my Facebook password so my Facebook messages would directly upload to my Twitter account. "How convenient," I thought as I typed in my password. "By Facebooking and Tweeting simultaneously I can kill two birds with one stone! Plus I want to build my Twitter followers up to as many as I now have on my Facebook friend list!"

The next morning, I woke to update my Facebook profile only to see that it had already been updated... by someone else, an intruder, and a hacker. A viral link stating, "Check out the funny video of me." had been posted to my profile wall. Rather than killing two birds with one stone I was now trying to kill the commotion on my Facebook page. While there is a real app for linking Facebook updates to Twitter, the email I had opened was spam. By gaining my password, the scammer was then able to post a virus on my wall to spread to all of my friends.

While I was still sleeping on Mountain Standard Time, my 1,500 friends, the majority of whom were on Eastern Standard Time and had gotten up two hours before me, had discovered the virus. A multitude of, "Rachel get this %$&^ off your wall, it's a virus" posts arrived before I even knew the link was there.

Their angry comments made me feel as if they thought I had purposely led my friends astray. Selfishly, I was less concerned about whether any of my friends had gotten the virus from my page than I was about whether my Facebook audience would shy away from clicking on my routinely embedded video links.

So what did I do? I went into overdrive uploading video links of myself in order to maintain my page's viewership. My equation of fearing defriending + over-sharing myself on Facebook = overcompensating is humiliating to me now.

My immoral compass continued to steer me to my wall no matter how often the angel tried to lift me up and out of Facebook damnation. Instead of basking in the success of my rejuvenated baking career, I kept getting "baked" on Facebook. I was stony baloney over social media.

While I yearned to break free of the site some of the time, I continued to make excuses to myself and Karl about how it was beneficial for networking and keeping in touch with friends. Just as we were shutting down our laptops one night Karl asked me, "How come you insist we close our curtains every night so our neighbors don't look in but you never worry about your friends looking into your life on Facebook while you sleep?"

Instead of admitting that I did worry about it, but that I couldn't help myself, I spewed out a couple of smart ass supporting reasons why I continued to recklessly post even after my account was hacked. Holding two fingers up I rattled off:

"Reason NUMBER ONE: To bring laughter to my peeps! Come on, Karl. Take the video you shot of me outside the Coors Field stadium wearing that skintight, cleavage-baring t-shirt while I handed out greasy paper bags filled with hot nuts, doing my finest Chicago twang imitation while shouting, "Daaaa Cubbies are here. Dey like dere beers." That was a good one, right, Karl?" (He actually nodded!)

"Reason NUMBER TWO: To bring praise to my wall! Remember the "4/20" photo shoot you took of me spread-eagle mounting a chopper bike in my Daisy Duke short shorts while inhaling a joint in honor of "National Marijuana Day." That was a hoot!" (This example only got me a head shake "no.")

Foolishly, I had posted photos of me smiling in the "Mile High" city with my "baked" space cakes on display at a Boulder marijuana festival booth. I wanted to prove that what I was doing was legal in Denver, as I had a medical marijuana license, and even more importantly, I wanted to help spread the efforts to legalize marijuana, which just so happened to backfire on my wall. While I got a lot of thumbs up from my other marijuana-license holding friends, some of my friends and relatives with teenaged children loudly expressed how completely inappropriate they felt my weed postings were. Some even went so far as to post that they were blocking me as they didn't want their kids looking at my wall anymore. I wanted to cry "uncle" to their Facebook criticisms! Couldn't Karl and the others see I only wanted praise in the name of pot and my profile! *"They are the ones with pot paranoia, not me!"* I joked to Karl, but he didn't laugh.

Like a dog with its tail between its legs, I headed to bed in the hopes I would sleep through the night and fight the urge to sneak back onto Facebook that evening. Karl was 100% right in questioning my motivations on Facebook.

Why did I stoop into somewhat dangerous social media territory? Why did I awake in the middle of the night with an urge to peek on my friends' Facebook pages? Why did I talk about others via posts, and why did I post about other people's postings? etc. Why did I even post? Why did I drunk post? Why did I click on a link if I didn't know for sure it was safe and legit?

My vicious, cynical cycle of Facebook gossip never

seemed to end.

Or could it? Was I simply too busy making a living on Face-book rather than spending time in social reality? Is it just easier to go home and log key strokes rather than to stroke an actual person? For me, I decided, it was.

Plus, I felt as if I had nowhere I could turn to for help. And no one to talk to about my embarrassing addiction. I had become a closet Facebook voyeur. Instead, I simply told myself, "Get your shit together, Ruff. Everybody else is doing it (Facebook) and they aren't spiraling out of control."

CHAPTER EIGHT

Status: Rachel Ruff is no longer comparing herself to others

*"I always thought it would be better to be
a fake somebody than a real nobody."*
—Tom Ripley, from The Talented Mr. Ripley

i was mOrTified. And I was ashamed. Too ashamed to admit I had a problem. Sometimes I would make my Facebook visits while I was sitting on the potty scrolling through my new Facebook app on my iPhone in the fall of 2010. I would be so immersed in my friends' Facebook page updates that I would later discover rings imprinted on my hiney from having been seated on the cold porcelain throne for over an hour. Karl once warned me, when I finally reappeared from the latrine, "You're probably going to get hemorrhoids from Facebook-ing so long in there."

In the existentialist play *No Exit*, Jean Paul Sartre wrote, "Hell is other people." According to Sartre, we all want to be our own masters, yet we cannot be. We are ill-fated to need others, whether we want to or not.

We are on an egotistical quest to gain respect and even adulation from others. This was certainly true for me while on Facebook.

The irony of the newfound Facebook friendships with my former classmates was that they had looked to connect with *me*, the lonely girl who had once desperately searched for a seat with them in the cafeteria. Though my request to sit next to them had been rejected some twenty years ago, here I was accepting their friend requests so they could see how the ugly duckling with pimples had turned out. I wanted them to see how I had blossomed into a swan of social media, both on the inside and on the outside. My aspirations to be accepted by the popular kids finally came true twenty years later when I was friend requested by them on Facebook. However, their lives no longer appeared to be filled with the eminence I once thought they had.

The burning question I couldn't answer was "Why was I so intertwined with them on Facebook if I didn't envy their lives?" I think it was simply that I wanted to be liked, admired. Perhaps even adored. I wanted them to acknowledge that Rachel Ruff was cool.

I would do flybys over these former classmates' pages which boasted of baby showers, keg parties, mall excursions, and pig roasts. By doing so, I felt I was able to glimpse what might have been my own life's destiny had I followed suit and continued to live down the same rural Georgia country roads on which we all grew up together. But there was one classmate I always seemed to get stuck comparing myself to: a girl I knew from high school who I had nicknamed "Sally the Queen of Suburbia."

Case in point. One frosty fall morning, I simply could not muster the will to get out of bed. I tried using the tactic of reminding myself of my blessings through meditating: *You are loved, you are healthy, yadda yadda yadda.* But no matter how long I tried to chant another uplifting mantra, the positive affirmations were not helping and I was sinking deeper and deeper into the down comforter. Even more frustrating, I was distracted from my meditation by the devilish voice in me wondering what I should post as my Facebook status for the morning.

Bullishly, I skipped a noon yoga class that probably would have boosted my low serotonin levels and banished my PMS bloat. Instead, my only stretching exercise was reaching down next to the bed where my laptop lay idle from my midnight Facebook monitoring.

As I logged onto Facebook, the news feed chirpily buzzed away with cheery nothings like "Happy Tuesday!" I began to feel the "FBs" kicking in, my nickname for the "Facebook blues" which was a true indicator of the severity of the side effects caused by my newly self-diagnosed Facebook addiction. And they were coming on strong. My husband and I had just moved into a new rental for the second time in two years because we didn't have any money left in our savings account to buy a house, our former lease was up, he was still unemployed, my career was flailing and the fact that I was PMSing wasn't helping. So

I sloppily typed after Rachel Ruff: "is PMSing BAD."

Dissatisfied with my PMS update, I deleted it and replaced it with a more clever posting, *"Mirror, mirror on the web, who's the fairest of them all?"* The next thing I did was look to see who did appear to be the fairest of them all.

There was a clear answer: "Queen Sally!" I sure as hell picked the wrong day to monitor her postings. Her latest post read: *"Miss the hubby, but we'll be together in the French Alps after my modeling shoot!"*

A minute later her darling, chiseled, and overly tanned hubby replied below her post: *"Luv ya tons."*

Who says that? I bitched to myself. When I witnessed significant others desecrating each others' walls with mushy messages, I always wanted to sarcastically post, "Luv ya tons too, but get a cyber-room will ya?"

Two hours later, I was still lying across the unmade master bed in my frayed and mustard-stained shabby robe with a red light flashing on my laptop warning me that my battery was low. Instead of getting up from the computer to break free from comparing myself to others, I jumped right back onto Sally's page. I discovered that "the Queen of Suburbia" was having an extremely lovely Tuesday overseas. *"Exhausted from shopping, heading out to get lunch and an amazing three hour massage."* It was like I had some kind of cruel mission to rub salt into my self-inflicted social media wounds and keep on waiting to see what the next fabulous addition to her day would be, rather than try and start a new day for myself.

Thirty minutes later. *"The McDonalds in Paris rocks!*

I'm washing the fries and Le Big Mac down with a chocolate shake." After Sally posted the massage and the McDonalds updates, she garnered several responses below them: *"Oh I so wish I had your life! And your bod!"*

After her fast food comment, which I bet was a crock of shit anyway, a gal pal posted, *"Honey, you need to eat like ten more, you're sooooo skinny!"* Minutes later, she jumped back onto her profile and graciously responded to her devoted followers' comments. *"Love you guys and dolls, get your ski boots packed for the French Alps this weekend! Can't wait to see you XOXO."*

During the four years I was on Facebook, I received several compliments from "Queen Sally" as well as many other male and female former classmates about my appearance. "Wow! Rachel, you turned out pretty hot!" Yes, these were the same students who had once shunned me in the high school cafeteria and at the stadium on Friday night football games when I asked to sit with them. So there was my validation, right?

Wrong. I just moved on to asking myself more insecure questions such as, "I wonder if they think I'm a loser because they found out I still rent an apartment while they own big houses?" and "Can't Sally see I want to go skiing with them too? After I had just posted below her Paris updates "Been too long, Sally, let's do a trip together! xoxo"

"Why has she responded to her other peeps but not responded to me? Aren't I cool enough? Can't she see that I have as many Facebook friends as her now?" I ruminated.

My inner sixteen year-old self was still hungry to

confirm that the old cafeteria table-shunners were now authentic in their "liking" of me but her lack of a response to me verified we were never close nor would Facebook bring us closer. Heck, did I really think I would get along with them?

Silently, a tear spilled onto the keyboard because that secret wish for closer ties within my Facebook friend relationships never came true. To express a hint of the pain I was in, I posted a verse from Madonna's 2002 hit single, "Die Another Day" later that afternoon. My message "Rachel Ruff: just died another day" was crystal clear to me, as I felt I was slowly dying a digitally inflicted death. But my status update completely bewildered my "friends" as was evident in their comments below my posting, "What?" "Are you dying?"

I squeezed tightly onto the little stuffed Piglet, I had named Pig-gee, whom I had slept with for years. No matter how pilled his fur had become or how old I was and even when I had Karl in my bed now, I could never "de-friend" the little guy. Pig-gee had remained beside me during my darkest days and my adventures too. And of course he had appeared in dozens of photos with me as my sidekick. I had tried to make Pig-gee a Facebook sensation on my wall. Here are a few Pig-gee postings:

> *"Pig-gee is going to Kansas to meet Grandpa and Grandma"*
> *"Pig-gee is celebrating the Chinese New Year! Its the year of the Pig!"*
> *"Rach-ee and Pig-gee are in bed with the flu"*

Just like his mother, Pig-gee never received the recognition I thought we both deserved. Instead, he was often unfairly attacked with friends' comments below his postings like, *"Put that dirty pig to sleep and out of his misery!"* Or *"How old are you, Rachel?! You still sleep with a stuffed animal?"* And as I read Pig-gee's unjust responses, I was reminded of how I hid my "real" self, choosing to hide my imperfections to my Facebook friends in the fear that if I was "found out" I wouldn't be liked.

Three hours later, my husband, the one person with whom I knew it was safe to be "real," and who loved me unconditionally, came into the bedroom to check on me. There I was, still moribund in our disheveled bed, which I should have made hours ago.

My spirit was just as drained of energy as was the laptop zapped of all its battery power from feeding my Facebook fanaticism. Once again, I was embarrassed that Karl was witnessing me completely bedraggled, clutching tightly to Pig-gee and crying over what I considered to be everyone else's seemingly marvelous lives on Facebook. I was FOMO'd and fucked up over Mr. Facebook once again.

Karl pulled me up as if I were a stray kitten, by the hood of my robe, loosening my mangy pig from my tight clutch and replacing Pig-gee with a mug filled to the brim with French press coffee and the cinnamon sprinkles I loved. He then handed me my favorite running gear, gave me a great big hug and said, "Oh honey, fuck Facebook." *He must have sensed that whatever I am crying about has to do with Facebook, without me even telling him!* As I laughed through my tears, I laced up my running shoes.

With each stretch of pavement I pounded, I praised myself for getting off the site and out the door. Sure, I learned things about people from their wall updates that I wouldn't otherwise be privy to, but was I learning anything meaningful or worthwhile? How does a friend's status that reads, "Washing my dog in the tub right now" enrich my life? *Come on, Rachel, you are better than that.*

As I shuffled through the leaves, I wondered to myself, *why don't I just rake in my friends and collect them up at a coffee shop? Piling up the love to jump into rather than diving into Facebook? And how have my Facebook friends helped to make me a better person through spreading their replies and thumbs ups across my polluted page? Are they true friends or are they "Fake-book" friends? What exactly was I willing to sacrifice for Mr. Facebook?* These were the questions that kept rattling around in my brain.

After my rejuvenating run, I took a long bath and returned to my recharged laptop to check out what I had missed on Facebook during my exercise break only to discover I had no new friend messages waiting for me except for one from my guardian angel. This time the angel didn't tap me on the shoulder either.

She had literally dropped an answer to the questions I had asked during my long run, in the form of Ralph Waldo Emerson's words. I had taped one of his quotations on the side of my computer desk several years ago, and when I opened the desk hutch, the weathered sheet of paper, which I hadn't looked at in ages, fell into my lap and was now staring straight up at me. I read the words of the quote again, and they took on new meaning.

> *"To laugh often and much, to win respect of intelligent people and the affection of children, to earn the appreciation of honest critics and endure the betrayal of false friends, to appreciate beauty, to find the best in others, to leave the world a bit better, whether by a healthy child, a garden patch...to know even one life has breathed easier because you have lived. This is to have succeeded!"*
> —Ralph Waldo Emerson

In that moment I decided I was going to get to the bottom of why I was letting Facebook cause me such anxiety and grief and really *hear* the meaning of his quote.

Emerson's words began to serve as a checklist for my social media activity. Had wise old Emerson been alive in today's world, I wonder if he would have added, *"To have used your Facebook account to help others."* Here's how I looked at my checklist.

"To laugh often and much" Nope, I cried while on Facebook.

Is Facebook a source of entertainment or anxiety? Do I agonize over my status updates? Does reading my friends' posts make me laugh or cause me envy or resentment? Yup.

"To win respect of intelligent people and the affection of children." Nope. I had lost their respect and gained anxiety over the

fact that my postings and photos were possibly viewed by the children of my friends and feared I would corrupt their kids.

If I looked back at all my posts, how many of them caused me embarrassment? Do my FB posts reflect the best of me? The real me? Nope.

"To earn the appreciation of honest critics." Nope, I would become upset and defensive when a caring family member or friend would kindly advise me to remove some of my lascivious pictures. Who are my critics? Are they honest critics? Had I earned their appreciation? Nope.

"To endure the betrayal of false friends" Negative! I wallowed in my own self pity when I discovered that I had been de-friended or negatively posted about. Do I want to be on Facebook because I want false friends? Am I strong enough to endure betrayal? Nope.

"To appreciate beauty." Heck no. I envied others' seemingly picture perfect walls and lives. What was beauty on Facebook to me? An old high school friend's profile picture of her new boob job spilling out of a bikini...A colleague's mansion which kept reminding me that I was just an apartment dweller...the dazzling Parisian vacation photos I discovered on a friend's wall, who had recently told me she didn't have travel money to visit me, neglecting to mention her overseas plans? Nope.

The final lines of the quotation really hit home

hard: "*To find the best in others, to leave the world a bit better, whether by a healthy child, a garden patch...to know even one life has breathed easier because you have lived. This is to have succeeded!*"

I couldn't even muster the word "Nope" on this one because I was crying my heart out. Facebook had been my sun, in which the only light shining upon me resonated from the glow of the computer screen. I yearned to get my soul outside, to reignite my gardening and my painting passions and most importantly, to keep away from the keyboard and the digital darkness. Rather than playing more childish games of break-up and make-up with Mr. Facebook, I wanted to set up play-dates with old friends and their toddlers whom I had only seen in Facebook ultrasound photos.

Just when did my euphoria with Facebook turn into a state of digital dysphoria? All of the little things that gave me such joy in life, like spending uninterrupted time with Karl, oil painting, gardening, or going to brunch with friends, I had pushed away to pursue my warped passion for posting. After drilling myself with those tough questions, my ultimate response was, "I have a Facebook Addiction. I have to quit!" For four forlorn years, I lived, no, I decayed, on Facebook. With each new day I had become increasingly immersed in my Facebook Pollyanna postings. The post-Emerson assessment signified to me that the angelic inner voice had finally won over my devil's digital desires. Did this mean I had truly "accepted" my mortality on Facebook? *Nope.*

CHAPTER NINE

Status: Rachel Ruff: Your Facebook Account Has Been De-Activated

*"I'm selfish, impatient and a little insecure.
I make mistakes, I am out of control and at times hard to
handle. But if you can't handle me at my worst, then you sure as
hell don't deserve me at my best."*
—*Marilyn Monroe*

almOsT a year afTer EmersOn's quOTe was miraculously dropped into my lap, I still hadn't quit Facebook and I was still grappling with the final stage of my Facebook death: acceptance. The Latin root word "cept" means "taken." This root word gives rise to the English term "accept," for when you have "accepted" something, you have "taken" it towards yourself. I had taken in many Facebook friends, about 1,500. But what had I given to them? And what had Mr. Facebook and them taken from me? I was about to get a tough-love answer from my angel in the fall of 2010. One of my fair-weather friends was about to take the last ounce of willpower I had for staying in my self-abusive relationship with Mr. Facebook.

I opened my inbox one early November morning to discover that my friend Cindy had sent me an email asking me to RSVP to a Facebook invitation to attend an art gallery party. The trouble was, the event happened to fall on the very same night I was hosting an intimate dinner party and had already sent out Facebook invites to a few of our mutual friends.

Cindy had always been sweet to me, but to the point of being sickeningly so, as was evident in her frequent ass-kissing Facebook messages to my wall like "Love you, baby!" and "How's my honey? Wasn't last weekend so much fun together!?" even though we weren't that close of friends and had simply run into each other on occasion.

After hemming and hawing to Karl over how I should politely respond to Cindy's invite, and already feeling awkward for not having included her on the Facebook dinner party invite, I sent her a succinct Facebook response, "Sorry, Karl and I will be out of town." So much for the social media spiritual awakening with Emerson's message on the importance of goodwill to all.

I felt guilty for lying and was engulfed with anxiety over the fear that she might find out. As I unloaded groceries on the day of my party, I glanced over at my laptop to discover my Facebook page was filled with a surplus of Cindy postings, "Are you in the mountains?" "Drive back for this amazing party." One hour later, "Party is going to be so cool." "Can't wait to see you!" Ten minutes later, "Beautiful girl, you have to be there!" A half hour later, "Hey gorgeous, I need to see your sweet face tonight. Please come."

I worried that my strategy of not responding to Cindy's postings might fail miserably. Just as I had sweated over the potential Facebook Vegas elopement drama, I automatically began to fret that one of my invited dinner party guests might spill the beans about the dinner party. "I can just see it now, a social media circus is about to ramp up on my wall, with RACHEL RUFF'S SHIT SHOW as the starring act," I moaned to Karl who poured me a glass of wine to stop my whining.

Twenty minutes later, as the meatballs I had made for dinner were marinating, I checked on my Facebook newsfeed to discover, "Chef Ruff can't make it because she is hosting an amazing dinner party tonight! I can't wait to sample her gourmet cooking." To which Cindy immediately responded, "You suck, Rachel."

To say I went ape-shit is an understatement. In my opinion, the dinner guest of mine, who had taken the initiative to directly respond to her postings, wasn't doing it out of innocence. I had felt he was doing it out of "importance" in order to post evidence that he was in the know and was invited to my place. He was a friend whom I had de-friended and re-friended on almost a daily basis due to his improper postings about me along with his annoying and very public requests on my wall to "pump" his Facebook page so that, as he claimed, "Your single girlfriends will take notice of your gorgeous profile pic and friend me."

Ironically, he was also the one who had introduced me to Renee, the "shoe-lifter."

But my anger wasn't directed at Cindy, nor to my dinner guest with the long track record of Facebook fuck-ups. My rage was solely aimed at the owner of the Facebook wall, myself. The social media party slight I had given to Cindy was officially the straw that broke the camel's back. For once and for all, I had had enough of Facebook drama.

Where was this pent up anger coming from?, I wondered. The succinct answer was revealed to me, not by my angel, but by my inner child, who empathized over exactly how Cindy must've felt.

By choosing to ignore her on my wall, I realized I was acting just as callous as the cool kids who had decided to ditch me on the playground during games of Red Rover and now on the French Alps ski trip too. I had stooped to their level as the "wall shunner" too. Instead of dismissing my guilt, my inner voice's nagging followed me into the dining room, even as the guests began to arrive at our home. With my laptop still logged into Facebook and close by the dining room table in order for me to peek at and monitor any new pissed off postings by Cindy, I somberly ushered our guests to their assigned seats.

Thirty minutes into our dinner party, I, the doyenne of digital drama queens, clinked my fork against a crystal goblet. Once I gained the attention of my husband and my friends, I blurted a startling announcement. "Rachel Ruff is going off of Facebook life support. Yeah, I quit." I felt like a weight had just been lifted from my shoulders with my admission.

But rather than applause, the room filled with hoots of laughter and my guests' responses of, "Yeah right, Rach." "You are so funny." "Have you had too much wine?"

No one believed me, not even my husband. I had no supporters, only doubters. I wanted to fling a meatball at each one of them. But instead, having assumed my new role as a Facebook tee-totaler, I left them to their gossip.

As their dinner table conversations skipped back to the typical theme of Facebook gossip like, "Did you see that slutty pic Megan posted on her wall?" and "What in the hell was she wearing?" I found that cleaning the kitchen and washing dishes suddenly felt more fulfilling to me than talking Facebook filth. Mr. Facebook was like a boyfriend all of my friends approved of and hung out with, not knowing that I was secretly harboring immense pain and anxiety over my unhealthy obsession with him. I had finally decided that the love/hate relationship with Mr. Facebook was too toxic for me to pursue, whether they believed me or not. I was throwing in the technology towel, with the hopes that during a weak moment of missing Mr. Facebook I would stay strong and not rebound.

While I had often felt like a loser online, by quitting the site I feared that people would think I was a Facebook failure too. "A winner never quits and a quitter never wins, right? Stay in the game, Ruff!" the devil taunted.

My social media angel softly whispered back, "Rachel, you are a lot of things. A perfectionist, a dreamer, oversensitive, impatient, loving, but one thing you are NOT is weak. You are doing a very positive thing for yourself. Who cares what the others think!"

The next day, the wintery cold and grey morning of November 16, 2010, I followed my angel's guidance and I pulled the plug on Facebook. For over an hour, while I sat dumbfounded trying to figure out how to quit Facebook via the complicated instructions in the tricky settings section, I kept replaying the angel's and the devil's opposing messages in my head.

Finally, after an arduous amount of clicking on the wrong links that I thought would guide me to deactivate my account, I discovered a new Facebook message in my Gmail inbox. The subject line read: "Your Facebook account has been deactivated."

In my opinion, the email header should have read: "Your life has been re-activated." As a coping mechanism or perhaps because I was totally cuckoo from the deactivating my account efforts, I picked up our stainless steel soup ladle and goofily pretended it was a mirror, like Stuart Smalley used in the old "Daily Affirmation" skits on "Saturday Night Live." I held it up to my face and then cheekily smiled into the shiny spoon reflection of myself, "I'm good enough, I'm smart enough, and doggonit, people like me!" before packing up my clothes to visit the only place I knew would be free of Facebook temptations, the yoga room at my fitness club in Denver.

I put down the ladle, pulled off my bathrobe and lifted my spirit out of the dumps and into reality. Instead of staring at my friends' photos on Facebook, I headed out of the computer room to manifest my soul among society rather than bury it within social media. I had also made a vow to myself to limit my time on other social media sites in order to prevent replacing one addiction for another. I sure didn't want to become a torrid "tweeter" on Twitter as a coping method. But how would I handle Facebook withdrawal? *How* and *when* might withdrawal pains set in?

Quickly, I discovered. After all, my death on Facebook came more like a heart attack than a slow arduous fight with cancer. I quit cold-turkey. *Bam!* Rachel Ruff is gone from Facebook. It's not like I weaned myself away by decreasing my posts from an average of about 20-30 a day to one to two a week to none at all and finally to de-activating my account.

Heck no, just as I did eloping with Karl or fighting for my job at CNN and K Street, I went for it. Some might call me impulsive, I call me intuitive.

Regardless, I soon found that ceasing Facebook life support was much more difficult than ripping off a Band-Aid because, in some twisted way, I felt like a failure for not being able to handle the heat on the social media site. The sting from dealing with the withdrawal pains of my social media sores seemed to grow more excruciating by the minute. And my wine-induced headache from the previous night's party wasn't helping ease my anxiety either.

I put my first Facebook-free hour to good use on my yoga mat, tackling challenging yoga poses and reconnecting with yogi community members. The hardest pose for me to master while active on Facebook had been "shavasana" which in Sanskrit means "corpse pose," a position where one lies in stillness and in silence. I had struggled with it for years because all I used to think about during class was what witty post I should write when I got home to show off that I just performed yoga. Something like, "Rachel Ruff loves doing the wind removing pose after eating chili." Gross. How sick I used to be. Now I would have to work on silencing my "quitting Facebook fears" in order to finally have the chance to come back to life on my yoga mat and master the pose with a calm mind.

True yogis don't show off. "Yoga is not only what you do on your mat but also what you do off of your mat," my instructor would always remind her students. I was finally on my way to learn how to become proficient in poses rather than posts.

During that first hour off Facebook and on my yoga mat, I studied the behavior of some of the most peaceful meditators in class. And I recalled how several of those yogis I admired were not on Facebook.

Two years before, when I first began practicing yoga, I had asked my yogi friend Becky, whom I admired immensely for her inner focus while on and off of her yoga mat, to friend me on Facebook. To which she had peacefully replied, "Sorry, Rachel, I'm not on Facebook. It is too noisy."

While Becky and I were splayed out upside down in the "downward dog" position side by side on our yoga mats that first Facebook-free morning, I confided to her in a mouse-like tone, "Becky, I quit Facebook this morning cold turkey." She reached over, and balancing on one hand, placed her free hand over one of mine and gave it a big squeeze.

I looked over at her from an awkward vantage point and realized that her and Karl's resistance to joining social media sites was not topsy turvy at all. Then I whispered to Becky, "Just because I dropped off of Facebook, I am not alone, am I?" She answered me with a soft "Shhh," as I watched her lie down and close her eyes, disappearing into "shavasana." I had no doubt she was deep in meditation chanting a special prayer for me to stay strong. I could feel her positive energy as I lay down alongside of her. Healthy release in the form of soft tears from years of locked up pain began to trickle down from my closed eyelids onto my cheeks as I soaked up her healing light.

Becky and Karl were right. There was noise on Facebook. A ringing in my ears. While I tried to justify the angel's heeds, I was always lured back to Mr. Facebook by my digital devil who would sway me with denial of my addiction. I had been on a runaway bus heading straight to Facebook hell. And thankfully, I had decided to jump. Now that I had escaped, I hoped I could survive without my ex.

CHAPTER TEN

Status: Rachel Ruff: Your Facebook Account Has Been Re-Activated

*"Advance, and never halt, for advancing is perfection.
Advance and do not fear the thorns in the path,
for they draw only corrupt blood."*
—Khalil Gibran

On nOvember 18, 2010, just two days after I had quit Facebook, I checked my inbox and saw that I had received an uncharacteristically high number of new email messages. I swallowed hard as I discovered most of the subject headers read "New Facebook message." My gastric juices were churning and quickly rising into my throat as I bent over my laptop to inspect the emails even closer. Had I unknowingly re-activated my Facebook account? *I have chugged along for an entire two days of forgoing Facebook. No surfing, no snooping, no scavenging, no nothing and now this?*

Furious, I stomped around the kitchen slamming cabinets while not even pausing to take in the breath-taking mountain views of the fresh snowfall from the night before. I was too busy creating my own stormy setting to observe the ethereal outdoor vista. I was confused and super-duper peeved. And I was even more upset that a stupid website was making me this upset.

My husband tiptoed in to see what the fuss was all about. But I didn't even notice him enter the room because I was loudly yelling "Fuck Facebook! Fuuuuuuuck Facebook."

He firmly grabbed me by the shoulders and said to me, as if he were talking down a suicidal stranger, "Honey, if you are going to be this bitchy because you miss your usual routine of sipping coffee in your bathrobe while surfing on Facebook, then just keep your account."

"No, Karl," I tartly replied, "the reason I'm bitchy is because I am still 'active', as in, my Facebook account is still online."

"Well, honey," he replied, "don't beat yourself up, there are worse things to be addicted to in this world."

Usually I adore Karl's sunny morning persona and I completely admired the fact that he never got caught up in the Facebook phenomenon. But on this day, when he reached out to give me a hug, I was so irate that I lurched away from his open arms. Thank God we don't have a cat, because I probably would have kicked the fur ball, too.

I snarled, "I'm pissed off because I thought that I had finally figured out how to quit Facebook." Pulling him to the laptop by his robe sash, I showed him the overwhelming pile of Facebook alerts that had filtered into my Gmail account overnight. As I continued to scroll down the sixty-plus new Facebook emails, I felt my spine tingle as I discovered an email with a disturbing header, "Your Facebook account has been re-activated."

"How in the hell has my Facebook account been re-activated?" I shouted at Karl before I read the contents of the email to him:

Hey Rachel,

The Facebook account associated with rachelsruff@gmail.com was recently reactivated. If you were not the one who reactivated this account, please visit our Help Center (http://www. facebook.com/help/?topic=security).

Thanks,

The Facebook Team

Karl threw up his hands. "I don't know how Facebook works, honey. What do you want me to make us for breakfast? Why don't you relax by the fireplace and look out at the beautiful snowfall?" *Typical man, he's trying to "fix" something rather than console me,* I thought to myself.

Rather than take my ire out on him by responding, "How 'bout you make me a cup of shut up?" I took the high road and ignored his questioning. I then got busy fighting my demons by deleting some of my former Facebook friends' messages, which all contained nearly the same dramatic verbiage: "Oh, Rachel, thank God you are still on Facebook, I went to your page the other day and it was gone" and "I thought you were dead or something terrible, like you de-friended me!"

For better or worse, I played dead. I sent no email responses or excuses back to any of them about why my page went missing. While Karl sizzled up bacon and pancakes on the stove, I sipped a fruit smoothie that I wished he had spiked with Xanax to calm my nerves.

Finally, after an hour of not being able to figure out how my account was reinstated, I decided to do something I rarely did when I was active on Facebook. I picked up the phone and rang a Facebook-savvy friend, a friend who had been there for my grand announcement at dinner two nights before. I was a bit uneasy because I was not used to making the extra effort to reach out to someone via phone. I sensed that my friend, too, was shocked to see my name on his caller i.d. as I had only called him once before.

Just when I thought his telephone was going to connect me to his voicemail, I heard his voice. In a bewildered tone, he answered, "Rachel?"

"Tim! You busy?" I nervously blurted.

"No, I'm just surfing around on my computer," he replied.

"Ugh, yeah sure. You mean, you are on Facebook."

My suspicion proved true, as he had already seen my page was back up.

"Rachel, for God's sake! Come on, you knew you weren't going to be able to keep away from being plugged in. Facebook is your lifeline. I'm surprised you even managed to stay off for this long."

Okay, no help there. I abruptly ended the call and went back to figuring out the social media reversal by myself. Even though I had once left Karl on his own to delete his account that I had guilted him into creating, I was desperate for help, so I called him back into the kitchen. But he was of no assistance, either.

"God dammit!" I yelled at my little laptop as Karl stood slack-jawed next to me. I was not about to become that scaly social media sucker on Facebook again. No one was going to suck me back onto Facebook. I thought about tossing my laptop over the balcony because I was so overwhelmed with all of the shallow and insincere Facebook messages and with Mr. Facebook trying to sneak back into my life. But then I stopped myself, took some deep yoga breaths and got busy trying to deactivate the account once again.

The answer finally came to me when I scrolled through my Gmail account and revisited an old email Facebook had sent me two days before. It read:

Hi Rachel,

You have deactivated your Facebook account. You can reactivate your account at any time by logging into Facebook using your old login email and password. You will be able to use the site like you used to.

Thanks,

The Facebook Team
Sign in to Facebook and start connecting (Link)

"Holy shit Karl! I must've accidentally clicked on an old email with an embedded Facebook link when I cleaned out my emails the night before. Those sly

Facebook web programming tools have tricked me once again."

With Karl still standing loyally by my side for support, I hurriedly expedited my RE-deactivation of my Facebook account before anyone else could slip me a post that I might want to take a hit of…I mean, a peek at. There was no way in hell that I was going to allow myself to get digitally drunk again after this accidental Facebook re-activation.

But first, before re-shutting down my account, I took a peek at one page. No, I did not take a hit of a friend's page that I used to be obsessed with. Instead, I decided to visit a page that I had never obsessed over before. But a page I truly should have combed through, starting on day one when I signed up with Facebook. I clicked on the registration terms page.

While reading the Facebook "terms of agreement" legal jargon, I discovered that even if I unwittingly hit an old ghost page link soon after my Facebook account had been deactivated, my page would become re-activated and visible to all. That is, unless I properly adjusted my privacy settings to disable that feature. I learned the hard way that YOUR ACCOUNT NEVER DIES.

The fact that I could never really quit Facebook was upsetting to me. But what I found equally frustrating was the fact that the Facebook settings didn't include an option for me to alert my friends that I had deactivated my account, not de-friended them. There was no such thing as a tool to let me put an update on the newsfeed reading, "Rachel Ruff went inactive on

Facebook."

I also realized after reading the fine print that I had been way too active with this digital-blind date-turned-obsession. Facebook states in the registration terms page that they own the rights to all of the photos I had uploaded to my account, even after I quit. I felt so used.

I thought by being in a relationship with his site, Mr. Facebook would in turn reciprocate the love, via helping promote my website and my catering business. Instead, I felt used as he whored out my pretty page, which was decked out to the nines with pink cupcakes and crisp apple strudel photos, to advertisers who placed competing catering and local bakery ads across the right side of my wall. If Mr. Facebook were a real-life boyfriend, I would have broken up with him much earlier than the four years it took for me to dump the social media scavenger.

He pimped me out and exposed my innermost private settings, even when I requested him not to divulge. He hiked up his Facebook company worth, while I hiked up my skirt for Facebook pictures. I felt his need to prove his company value to potential investors seemed simply too important a priority than for him to focus on chasing little ole me back to the land of loving Facebook. After all, I was just one in a BILLION users who were still active and deeply immersed in being asked to the digital dance on the Facebook ballroom floor.

To me, Mr. Facebook was like a boyfriend you abruptly break up with and delete from your cell phone after years of compromising your values to please him and then cringe wondering *Why did I ever "sext" him those licentious photos? Who will he show them too? Could he sell them to a soft porn site?* I had been putting out and he had taken advantage.

While I was emotionally exhausted, I felt invigorated after that accidental slip-up when he tried to get back together with me. My next task at hand was to cease my Pavlovian tendency to visit Facebook each time I drew near my keyboard, as I imagined an alcoholic's hand must do if one sat next to a cocktail before having completely finished a detox program. So I put my shaky hands to work by journaling about my journey from being a lover of Facebook to a pusher of Facebook to an addict of Facebook and, ultimately, to a de-friender of Facebook, in order to come to a deeper understanding of why I had experienced such emotional turmoil while using the site. My conclusion: I wasn't acting as the grown woman I truly and beautifully had become. The isolated teen the others had once ignored in school was still dwelling deep within me and completely vulnerable to the devil's messages. Once I wrote of that epiphany in my diary, the terrible curse of being addicted to Facebook became a sort of blessing as I began to appreciate the beauty of life off of Facebook. My thirty-five-year-old-self chose to heal her inadequacy woes and stop worrying about what others may *or may not* think of her. There is beauty in solitude I learned once again. At first, I was afraid being off Facebook would feel like the loneliness I felt at the cafeteria table. To my delight, I discovered instead it was a feeling of peace one experiences on a walk alone in a beautiful forest or a deserted beach.

In a sense, I felt my fear of being isolated if I quit Facebook meant I truly *did* need to be alone in order to embrace the real Rachel Ruff. Without having to "be" on Facebook, I no longer had to pretend to be someone I wasn't. I realized Facebook was not a reflective mirror I used to look within, but more of a carnival mirror within which I molded and twisted myself into the image I wanted to portray to others. I was in my own personal "hell is other people" while on Facebook because I was looking through a distorted mirror in which I couldn't see myself clearly.

Rearview mirrors in vehicles come with a warning sticker, "Objects are not as close as they appear to be." Those objects were my friends, but I couldn't see or accept that they weren't as close to me as I had imagined. I had to crash in order to make the discovery and escape from my hell, my wall. Having done that, I found that I no longer gave myself a look of disgust when I looked in a real mirror anymore.

I didn't hate Mr. Facebook anymore either. I simply realized we weren't suited for each other. He taught me things about myself that have made me a better person, and I hope a better friend. Most importantly, he taught me that my dignity and my self-love were things I would no longer sacrifice as public offerings in the form of photos and phony posts in order to be liked by Mr. Facebook.

Facebook had brought me both pain and pleasure. For a long time I tricked myself into believing that my obsession with Mr. Facebook was puppy love, not an addiction, and that those highs and lows were the sacrifices I would have to make in order to grow in my relationship with him and the Facebook friends.

By taking baby steps to reintegrate myself into the real world as I once knew it, I figured that I could reduce my risk of slipping. But would I fall prey to Mr. Facebook again? *No, not this time,* I thought to myself as I gazed up at the words of Emerson on my sticky note. I was determined to triumph over my social media addiction.

But I still felt as if I was missing one key component to further enrich my recovery. Who could write up a prescription for a Facebook cure? While counseling was a good start, even my regular therapist didn't seem to understand how addicted I had been. Nor did she have the name of a doctor who could treat my post-Facebook pains and phantom keyboard shakes.

So I became proactive and spent the rest of the week writing my own Facebook addiction prescription in the form of a five-step program similar to those created for other addictions.

The steps were just five simple mantras that I taped to the wall directly above my computer monitor and alongside the Emerson quote to serve as a daily reminder. Each time I sat down at the computer, I focused on one of my newfound mantras. I also gently reminded myself of all the grief I had endured while carrying on with Mr. Facebook.

Step One: I gently yet firmly acknowledge that I suffer from a social media addiction.

Step Two: I bravely admit that I am powerless over Facebook. My life has become unmanageable.

Step Three: I turn my will and my life over to the care of true friendships, as I understood them before Facebook.

Step Four: I seek to improve conscious contact with those less fortunate and in need.

Step Five: I continue to take personal inventory of my other online time wasters. I will properly admit to them as I have done with my Facebook addiction.

Uploading comments on Facebook had been easy. After I quit Facebook, processing why I had chosen to over-share so much was even more painstaking. My insecurity and inadequacy scars began to fade as I continued to gain a complete comprehension and an admission as to why I had experienced such emotional turmoil on Facebook by writing below each step what my underlying issues were.

I needed to step back and re-evaluate situations, relationships, and frankly, my life purpose in general. As I went through my healing period, I spent a lot of time alone as I worked to become my own best friend again. I went into hiding for a while to work on healing my scars. I spent precious time bonding with the little girl inside of me who had so desperately wanted friends. I needed to teach her the most important friend she had to become bonded with was herself, and assure her I wasn't going to let her rush back out in society to get in touch with friends and have true interactions again, instead of posting and instant messaging without doing the work within. That took me about one month of doing yoga and painting. And amazingly, my heart did not stop beating after processing the heartache, as I had feared. In fact, my heart began to soar as I realized I was going to have a hell of a lot more free time to spend in coffee shops sipping lattes sans a laptop and gabbing on the phone with long distance friends.

Even though I knew those Facebook words and photos I posted lived on, I was able to release the past and free myself in order to move on to new experiences. Or so I hoped.

Rather than grieving over my lost so-called Facebook friends, as the winter holidays were fast approaching, I chose to get busy playing "Little Miss Christmas" as the holiday is my favorite time of the year. The hardest part of preparing for the blessed season of the winter sans a Facebook account was the fact that taking Christmas photos of my tree-trimming and holiday pastry creations to post had been a major festivity for me. I now had no one except my husband, a few close friends, and my in-laws to witness my Christmas decorations and intricately-decorated cookies.

The year before, I had blinged out my Facebook wall, literally. A grand photo of my freshly manicured fingers donning a diamond-studded ring which I had inherited from my husband's father as a Christmas gift, and one of me seated at a fancy steakhouse in my furs and new ring at a holiday party, or the reindeer hairband which flashed red and green lights above my head, were just a few I used to up my Santa ante.

Belatedly I realized, "Real smart, Ruff, let's broadcast the jewels that we have now accumulated in our tiny apartment for potential thieves to read about." But this year I told myself I had learned my lesson the hard way, especially after our New Year's Eve robbery two years before. I was off of Facebook, which meant, hopefully I was also off potential Facebook robbers' radars.

I "ass-u-me"d incorrectly! My closet bandit reared her ugly head once again via an email to my husband. Her timing was impeccable. One wintery night, just a week before Christmas, my husband and I had just finished decorating the Christmas tree and were in jovial moods. He went to his home office to check emails while I prepared a giant pot of juicy Colorado buffalo chili and hot mulled and spiked cider.

As I hummed along to the holiday carols playing in the background, I diced and sliced garlic in my checkered apron, soft Victoria's Secret flannel pjs and warm, fuzzy red slippers. I was in heaven and completely unplugged from learning about others' Facebook holiday dramas. That is, until I heard my husband's unusually stern tone of voice.

Karl's office was just a room away from our kitchen. "Rachel, I need you to come in here," he called. I quickly turned down my gas stovetop to a simmer and padded into his office to see what he was simmering about.

He looked pissed as he turned his giant computer monitor screen to face me and said, "Read this." I had trained him well enough to know that when I am in chef mode and in the throes of cooking or baking, no one was allowed to disturb me. No one, except for my Facebook alerts back when I was active. So I assumed he meant serious business.

I was shell-shocked when I read the words on his screen. The New Year's thief whom I had busted, had decided to pay us a Grinch-like visit. After not having had contact with us for a year, she had decided to send my husband, whom she knew despised her, a threatening email. "If Rachel doesn't stop trash talking me, I am going to post a nude photo of her on everyone's Facebook wall."

I racked my brain and calmly responded to him, "Bullshit. I'm calling her bluff. I don't even think about her or talk about her. Honey, the only way she could have a nude photo of me is if she slipped into the bathroom while I was showering before a girls' night out when she came over early to meet for a predinner drink."

I then shivered and figured there could be a slight chance that she had a blackmail-like photo. I recalled that she had been in our master bathroom the night before the Halloween of 2008 when my Dior perfume and my Chanel hoop earrings seemed to have walked right off my bathroom counter top. So I couldn't put it past her to have snapped a steamy pic of me as I took a hot shower. "Perhaps this is payback for her one year anniversary of angst over the theft charges."

I needed to step away from the drama, but just as I crossed the office threshold to get back to the chili,

I spun back around on my slippers to face Karl and exclaimed, "Honey, that crazy bitch doesn't have a nude photo of me wearing only my skivvies. I remember now! She simply has a photo of a group of my girl pals and me posing from a staircase in my condo last Christmas. From the angle in which I had been framed, I remember that you could see a slight hint of my red and green underwear, as the photo was taken from below the staircase. I asked her to delete it from her camera."

Right then and there I decided I wasn't going to worry about her nude posting threats. After all, if she really did upload a nude picture of me on Facebook for all my old friends to discover, I'd have to keep the faith that the Facebook security team would give her a slap on the hand or threaten to deactivate her as they had done to me.

I headed back through the living room to admire the tree and took a sip of the delicious cider. I peeked back into Karl's office and caught a glance of my husband's lips curled into a smile and I heard him chuckle. I think he was proud of my pluckiness, and I was too.

Later that night, I learned from an old Facebook friend that Renee had just posted the revealing staircase picture of me with my panties peeking out from under my dress. But the best news I got from her phone call was that no one ever posted a comment under the annoying photo. Her credibility among our small social circle of mutual Facebook friends was so far shot and my friend said that most had immediately deleted the amusing panty shot from their walls.

An hour later, Karl finally came into the kitchen to slurp up his bowl of steaming hot chili, probably not completely sure of what kind of mood I'd be in, given the latest Facebook fiasco. But rather than throw a utensil or shout at my poor innocent Facebook drama bystander, which used to be my typical reaction, I raised my glass of wassail to him and said, "My name is Rachel Ruff. I am one month, three days and eight hours Facebook sober."

He sweetly yet sarcastically toasted back to me, "Thumbs up, baby doll." After we clinked glasses, my true love held me tightly in his arms. Right then and there, I counted my lucky stars as I knew I was safe from any more postings of intimate photos. Fa-la-la-la-la freedom at last! Had the "heart-to-heart" talk with my guardian angel finally sunken into my stubborn social media self? I was fed up with being burnt, hacked, attacked, and overexposed on Facebook.

After having struggled in vain to develop a healthy relationship with Mr. Facebook for over four years, the significant meaning behind Emerson's *This is to have succeeded* quote finally rang true. Little Miss Christmas was finally at peace with herself and officially broken up with Mr. Facebook. I was moving forward into my five-step program and I wasn't about to snowball back down this social media avalanche. I remained secure in focusing on Step Three.

Step Three: I turn my will and my life over to the care of true friendships, as I understood them before Facebook.

Status: Rachel Ruff is "The Real and Desperate Housewife" of Denver

*"I like nonsense, it wakes up the brain cells. Fantasy
is a necessary ingredient in living. It's a way of looking at life
through the wrong end of a telescope, which is what I do,
and that enables you to laugh at life's realities."*
—*Theodor Seuss Geisel*

There's sOmeThing else i shed after quitting Facebook; I lopped off fourteen inches of my long mane of blonde hair on December 29, 2010. I donated it to Locks of Love, a non-profit which makes wigs out of real hair for impoverished cancer patients. Subconsciously, I think I also chopped it off as an act of rebellion towards Mr. Facebook and so that I wouldn't have an urge to get Karl to take pretty pictures of my long flowing locks like I used to post on Facebook each week. Dumb idea. Karl didn't miss my Facebook banter, but he sure missed my hair!

I ran into a casual Facebook friend at the Whole Foods while stocking up for a quiet New Year's Eve

dinner with Karl and he half-jokingly said while looking me up and down, "No wonder you are missing on
Facebook. You cut off all your hair! By the way, I'm
not going to send you a happy birthday post this year
since you forgot my birthday yesterday!" To which
I half-heartedly responded, "Sorry. Guess I missed
the news flash. I'm not on Facebook anymore." His
response, "Lame excuse, Ruff." He truly didn't believe
me.

I wanted to say, "Jack, you are one of the reasons I
quit Facebook." Jack was infamous for snapping candid drunk pics of his friends and I was often the vic-
tim of his posting pranks. Like the one of me, spread
out on a picnic blanket napping in white jeans with
red wine stains all over my pants from him when he
had stumbled over a cup and spilled it on me. Then I
would immaturely wait for the opportunity to pounce
and post a revenge photo of him. Like the time I captured a candid shot of Jack, pants down, urinating in
the middle of the day on my neighbor's front lawn and
posted it on his wall and mine for all of our thousands
of friends to see. When this back and forth Facebook
revenge posting became exhausting, I had to either
avoid parties where he was invited or stay up all night
waiting after a party to monitor his wall activity and
make sure he didn't have any digital dirt on me. Instead of arguing with him over Facebook cessation,
I pulled my scarf around my hairless neck and high-
tailed it out to the crowded parking lot to speed away.

During January of 2011, after Jack's jab in the parking lot, I realized that only three people out of my

1,500 friends actually reached out rather than just to inquire about my true whereabouts and reasoning for going off Facebook. One was an old friend of mine from CNN. Via a text message he wrote: "RR - you still alive?" I wrote back, "Just because I quit Facebook doesn't mean I'm dead." To which he replied, "Are you okay?"

I waited until I cooled my jets and finally wrote back a few hours later, "Am I okay?! I'm great!" Like me, my old friend had become a social media expert for a PR firm after he left CNN, and he must have thought I had lost my social media marbles. "So life is still good in the big D? You still married?" Once again, my history of over-sharing my ever changing relationship status came back to haunt me. "Yes" was all I wrote back and I haven't heard from him since.

The trouble was, I had almost forgotten how to reach out sans my postings. I was like a widow too insecure to jump back into the dating world and unsure of the proper etiquette. But I soon learned reconnecting was like riding a bike. You can pick right back up. Except I did have to put on training wheels for the face-to-face confrontations. No longer did I have to waste my time trying to decipher whether my witticisms were taken kindly or had been offensive. Instead, I had to look directly into a friend's eyes and express my sincere thoughts while listening to their genuine responses. No longer could I just hit delete or de-friend. I had to deal with them. Sometimes reconnecting in the real world was exhilarating but other times it was saddening. Not all of my friends' responses to my foray back to life and reality were positive. During those early weeks of my Facebook sobriety, I sometimes felt as if I were wearing the social media scarlet letter. Especially when a friend of mine confronted me in spin class and curtly asked, "Why haven't you commented on the baby photos I posted, Rachel? You used to post cute comments to my new pics all the time. Are you mad at me?"

I transformed my negative energy into sending a handful of friends, whom I truly missed on and off Facebook, emails listing three options to reach me. "Hey. I'm alive, all is good. I just decided to quit Facebook. Too many distractions on there for me. But I still love you and miss you so either: 1) call me, 2) text me, or 3) email me."

I guess I could have added an option 4) write me. But I assumed that the post office was something of the past for most of these stamp-less Facebook socialites, like I once was, so I wasn't going to hold my breath.

Heck, assuming that they even had my email, phone number or home address was even a leap of faith in itself. After all, I too had been so reliant on Facebook that a large portion of my friends probably didn't have my contact info, nor did I have theirs, nor their birthdays. Turns out not even half of them responded to inquire about my contact information. When I quit Facebook at the end of 2010, 608 million people were active on the site, according to the Associated Press. People must have thought I just dropped off the face of earth. Facebook was exploding at the exact time

I went extinct, which must have seemed a bit odd to friends. But it was time.

Within just a few weeks, I found I was better able to love myself, to be myself, and most importantly, I was proud of the fact that I was now hungry to be of service to others, rather than to serve as my friends "designated Facebook Pollyanna poster." I was no longer a player in the Facebook fame game either. I was one and a half months, one day, and twenty minutes Facebook sober.

Happily, as time went on I increasingly found myself cultivating friendships with people I knew from the gym or the neighborhood who I realized had given up asking me to hang out thanks to my lackadaisical friendship formula at the time: No Facebook account = Digital Dark Age member. "Going to lunch with Kelly" posted to my wall was more important back then than actually going to lunch and enjoying the company of a friend with true sincerity like I do now. No announcement to others needed.

Something even more exciting happened, too. Out of the blue, my old friend Shelly from my awkward teenage years rang me. I had moved three times in my four years of high school which never helped boost my popularity. She was in the cool crowd at the first high school I had attended yet would usher me to weekend activities like sleepovers in order to help me gain approval with her clique. I had always been in awe of her. Even though her attempts to score me points in the popularity contest failed miserably, we remained in touch over the years, sticking together as pen pals. I could confide in her about my loneliness in my ever-changing classrooms. And she in return would sarcastically write letters back praising my nerdy-ness. When I answered her unexpected call, I discovered she hadn't changed that much and I recognized her voice immediately.

"Hey, Rach, am I going have to come over there and kick the shit out of you?" "Come over from where, Shelly? Kick the shit out of me for what!?" I said.

"From Colorado Springs! I couldn't tell you I moved because you're off Facebook."

I love Shelly, she's a hoot. Why has it taken us this long to reconnect? I wondered after finally getting off the phone with her two hours later.

Sure enough, Shelly visited me in Denver the very next week. We had a great time catching up and as a bonus, she didn't kick my butt for getting off Facebook as she threatened. Instead I told her of my ongoing journey toward tending to my social media scars. Just as she had done as my little pen pal twenty years before, she used her wicked humor to help me realize that even if some friends don't understand my problem or as she put it, "think that I am a freak of nature," that they will love me on or *off* Facebook.

To celebrate the relief that my dog days of Facebook were over in February, I decided to get myself a true best friend. As in, man's furry four-legged companion: a doggie. My mother-in-law was quite impressed that I had quit Facebook and as an avid animal lover, she took me to a nearby pound to help me pick out a dog. Everyone always said the right one will just come up to you and you'll know. Well. Not one came up to me.

My husband knew of my frustration and started to help me look for a puppy online. He said he'd prefer for our dog to come from a good breeder and shared a link with me. I spent hours on the breeder's site he had found. Her dogs were almost too perfect. They were so adorable. They could have starred in a Purina commercial. And then I saw him. He was the one.

I wanted to look on the breeder's Facebook doggie page to get more glimpses of the pup. But I decided to steer clear of the fan page link she provided.

According to the seller, the one I fell in love with was a puppy fresh from a new litter. Her dogs seemed to get the word "SOLD" posted so quickly over their adorable website photos, that Karl and I, caught in a moment of emotional rather than rational response, transferred her the $1,000.00 amount she had put on him to her PayPal account. Before we even met him, to commemorate my three-month newfound Facebook freedom, I named my puppy Bodhi. Translated from Buddhism in English the word means "enlightened" and literally means "awakened." The trouble was, Bodhi and I never did get to meet.

Bodhi, we later learned from the Better Business Bureau, was probably not real but instead was a digital scam of dog photos she had pulled from a real breeder's Facebook page and posted to her bogus company website, as many online dog breeder frauds have been doing.

Unfortunately, Karl had stumbled onto a bogus breeder's website. I was now Facebook-less, dog-less, and as if things couldn't get worse, I was about to become shoe-less. I felt hopeless.

I had been logging many miles running in the time I had previously been wasting on Facebook. As I ran, I felt the wind beneath my website-free wings. After having freed up my Facebook time, I had gone into full-time barefoot fanatic running shoe mode on the concrete paved running trails through Denver. Then, one day in March 2011, I felt a snap. I broke two metatarsals in my left foot.

No more running for a few months until the fractures healed, the doctor ordered. She also confined me to the couch for a month, not even permitted to walk around in a boot brace for the first week. With no puppy to pet or Facebook to post to, I felt lost. But I was not going to retreat to Mr. Facebook to distract me or to find friends from which to attract sympathy and attention.

When my $400.00 boot was finally prescribed, in order to cheer myself up, I decorated the ugly black brace with a bunch of sparkly shamrock stickers in honor of St. Patrick's Day. As I humbly blinged out my handicapped foot, I recalled how I had participated in a St. Patrick's Day Shamrock Race in downtown Denver the previous year, a running event that was renowned for the outlandish costumes participants wore and the always unexpected and quickly changing weather patterns in which it took place.

My "Grama Sam" as I called her, was 100% Irish Catholic and boy, did she take her green beer celebration seriously. Especially after she received the gift of a long-awaited kidney transplant on St. Patrick's Day of 1983, when I was in the third grade. She had been afflicted with the debilitating onset of polycystic kidney disease. Though her transplanted kidney had functioned well for almost two decades, quite a medical miracle, her loving heart wore out from the transplant medications and she died of a massive heart attack when I was twenty-six years old.

On that 27th anniversary of her blessed kidney transplant celebration, I had defamed her favorite holiday. Amidst a flurry of snow and a sea of green-beaded pavement pounders, I had been decked in a tight Kelly green tee shirt, a shiny green shamrock beaded necklace, and a ridiculously short and fluffy white crinoline with green and white striped stockings peeking out from underneath. I had also made sure to stand out with a pair of neon purple Nikes, because that was my deceased grandmother's favorite color. The highlight of my costume was a long, sexy, red wig that I tied up in ponytails and green ribbons.

At the starting line, I shivered in the Colorado springtime sleet with wind gusts ranging over 40 mph. Though I was completely underdressed, the climate was not my concern. The anticipation of how cute I'd look for my Facebook profile was all that mattered to me. At the end of the race, my husband, who avoids crowds with a passion, was standing at the finish line with open arms for his frigid, half-Irish lassie.

But rather than savor the moment of seeing him cheering me on, my main concern was to make sure his loving arms held the camera with which I desperately wanted him to capture a winning photo of me for my profile picture.

While my husband Karl was there to support my running agility, I was there to support my Facebook popularity. Rather than exclaiming, "Thanks for coming, honey. Kiss Me! I'm Irish! Now let's enjoy the post-race St. Patty's day parade!" I was barking, "Gotta get back to the apartment. I need you to upload these pics to Facebook ASAP." He was living in the present, whereas I was living for my postings.

After I uploaded the race photos, recklessly choosing only the sexiest images, I proceeded to post, "Top of the Mornin' To Ya!" as my status and enjoy all the postings cheering me on while leaving Karl to cook the corned beef and cabbage by himself.

Sadly, I realized now, a year after the race, that when I had been active on Facebook, I had completely dispensed with the wise words my grandma had once said to me. When I was in high school she took it upon herself to impart some no-nonsense advice: "I want you to have fun, but remember you have to be careful, too. Be like your Grama Sam. Now, I wasn't as pure as the driven snow… but I wasn't the town whore either." I had taken her frank words to heart and let them guide me throughout college frat parties and beyond, but later I had become a Facebook whore. I was too busy posting how hot I looked to remember her warning to be careful too.

As I came back to reality on the couch, I turned away from the window to focus on the reality shows which I had been watching more and more to fill up my debilitating boot-legged days. I feared I would soon develop sofa sores from all of the dramas on television I was beginning to soak up. Reenlisting myself into the real world as a soldier fighting her social media battle had been going well until my battle-ship injury sank me into the couch.

Just because I had quit Facebook didn't mean I had become a social media saint. While I had unplugged myself from Facebook, I had not banned myself from all of the other social media time vacuums. I increasingly found myself turning to the tube for comfort, as in the television and YouTube. No, I wasn't on a National Geographic kick. I was out to get my Facebook drama fix in the form of reality shows.

My addiction transfer was fed by watching back-to-back episodes of the "Real Housewives of Beverly Hills", "The Bachelor", "The Playboy Mansion", "Kendra", and anything with the original "Real Housewife of New York" turned "Skinny Girl" Margarita tycoon, Bethenny Frankel.

Dr. Phil and Oprah show viewings were only during commercial breaks or on days when the reality episodes weren't juicy enough for me. Catching reruns to further analyze some outfit or plastic surgery was mandatory as well. These cast members became my replacements for my former Fake-book friends. Focusing on celebrity lives just the way I used to focus on friends' walls. I was replacing one crutch (Facebook) and substituting it for another (reality shows and gossip magazines) trying to sneak in some more "Fear Of Missing Out" time also known as FOMO by using my handicapped lifestyle as an excuse for slipping up on Step Four, by scoping and critiquing the rich and famous rather than focusing on helping those less fortunate and in need.

One of my favorite parts of my day was to limp down to the mailbox in the hopes of discovering the latest US Weekly subscription peeking out. I justified keeping my subscription up to date by telling myself that I was reading about how celebrities are just like us, even regarding their social media addictions. I read that Mick Jagger said, "I spend way to much time on the computer. It's easy to keep in touch with people... some of whom I wish I'd never kept in touch with. But there they are, on Facebook!"

I leaned on virtual counseling via Dr. Phil episodes about "Catfish" and teenage bullying. When Ellen featured the "IN YOUR Facebook" episodes they would always cheer me up by poking fun at some audience member's embarrassing profile pictures.

So yeah, maybe I no longer hit the computer first thing in the morning to read all of the Facebook updates I missed while sleeping, and hit my yoga mat instead, even when I was healing in my boot. Though I couldn't do the poses, I would join the yogis to soak up their healing energy while lying on my mat meditating. But sadly, what I did after wishing my fellow classmates a heartfelt *Namaste* was another thing.

My yoga bliss Zen rubbed off me as soon as I got in the front door of our apartment. Before I would even put the keys down, or the groceries on the counter, I did something definitely not peaceful, I turned on the

TV and remained parked in non-reality watching the reality shows and flipping through dirt in magazines.

I eventually got the boot off and began running again as summer arrived, and fortunately I no longer went running to the mailbox for my juicy gossip magazines. I even turned off the TV. Which wasn't as hard as I thought powering "off" would be. Especially after the reality shows began increasingly running "Like us on Facebook" and "Follow us on Facebook" commercials nonstop, I completely stopped liking them. I realized they were similar to the people whom I had followed on Facebook, nothing but drama. I was done having disjointed and shallow relationships, whether on Facebook with friends or on the tube with the "Fashion Police."

Besides, I had finally found myself a true and new friend. He wasn't on Facebook either. He did come with a price tag though. But one far less costly than my reputation. He cost me $3.00. He is a beautiful blue beta, or Japanese fighting fish, that I purchased on Cinco de Mayo. We never fight. When I sprinkle food in his Buddha fish bowl, I lovingly talk to Cinco, reminding him that I am "so happy you and me are free from Facebook."

Karl, Cinco, and I are like three peas in a pod. Though none of us are on Facebook, I post daily affirmations to them on the fridge chalk board for no one else to read but them. I thrive on sharing my love with Karl no longer waiting for the "like" button from strangers in return. I also post loving reminders to myself where my five-steps once hung, next to Emerson's quote. "Rachel Ruff: is one-year five days Facebook sober. And Rachel Ruff: has re-friended herself."

I cherish my safe and serene social network. And I think Karl relishes having my full attention. "It's 10 p.m. Do you know where your wife is?" was our joke when he would head off to bed as I would burrow in at my desk with Mr. Facebook. I no longer gossip about others at the dinner table with Karl, either. We actually sit down together and talk about productive things and I listen to his stories of the day. Towards the end of my time on Facebook, getting digital drunk no longer gave me a high. Just as alcohol is a depressant, so was Facebook when I got caught up in comparing myself to my Facebook friends. Dinner table conversation with my husband back then wasn't "honey, here's what I did today..." it was "here's what I read today about so and so on Facebook" while his eyes began to glaze over. To this day I'm surprised that he never yelled across the table to me, "Honey, get a life!" Or "Honey, get a real friend!" When I asked how his day was, I'd then interrupt him with some other trivial factoid I learned on Facebook before he could even finish his answer. "Honey, did you know that Carrie got a new hybrid car? She posted a pic of it on Facebook and it's an odd shape." Or "Oh my God, can you believe Tiffany drunk- posted last night?" I really didn't have anything else to talk about because the major chunk of my day was sadly spent looking to see what was happening on Facebook. If it wasn't posted on a wall, I didn't care.

Gossip is no longer permitted online or at our dinner table. Now Karl's eyes widen with interest when I divulge the technique I use to paint so many bees in my latest and greatest art accomplishment. Or when I tell him of the new art class I joined, and the sweet little old lady I met at the assisted living home where I volunteer who told me about her deceased husband's adventures in WWII.

Unfortunately, while I could shut out the noise on Facebook, I couldn't keep the "Like us on Facebook" signs out of my life. I struggled hard to keep myself calm and centered through the hot summer and fall of 2011 when Facebook seemed to be taking over the world. Grocery store placards which had bold prints reading "like us on Facebook." were big triggers. Because I am such a penny pincher and coupon queen, I often feared that I might relapse back onto Facebook by justifying that I was faced with no other option than to re-activate my account in order to save 20% on grocery purchases by liking a store or product.

By chanting my new mantra, "Fuck Facebook," I was able to use humor to deal with my one-day-off-Facebook-at-a-time struggles. But sometimes I grew wary of saying the crass four-letter word. So in order to keep the faith that I was doing the right thing, and to prevent caving in to Facebook peer pressure, I would just grumble "F-F" or "F to the F!" in between deep yoga breaths, which made me feel better and was also a much more appropriate coping mechanism when I was out in public.

Walking the aisles like a leper with a social media scarlet letter still fresh on my forehead, I would mutter to the signs, "Why don't you just like me OFF of Facebook." A cashier happened to overhear me grousing over this non-Facebook account-holding handicap of mine as I pulled out the cash from my wallet to pay for my non-Facebook discounted groceries. "Is everything okay, ma'am?"

"No it's not okay. What if I love your store, but I just don't like Facebook? Am I screwed out of the discount?" To my amazement, her lips curled into a smile and she punched in the 20% towards my bill. I could have kissed her.

In April of 2012, I was finally one-year and five months footloose and fancy free from Facebook! My focus was no longer centered on myself and how I appeared to others or how others' walls appeared to me. But instead I was focused on reactivating my third eye center, which the Hindus refer to as the gate that leads to inner focus and spiritual enlightenment, both in yoga classes and outside. Playing games like "Kick the Pigeon" on Facebook was replaced with perfecting the "pigeon pose" in yoga. By the end of fall, at my one year and one month and two day anniversary of quitting Facebook, people were beginning to experience me for who I truly was rather than what I appeared to be on Facebook. I checked step four off my list: *I seek to improve conscious contact with those less fortunate and in need* and moved on to focusing on the big finale. *Step Five: I continue to take personal inventory of my other online time wasters. I will properly admit to them as I have done with my Facebook addiction.*

CHAPTER TWELVE

Status: Rachel Ruff has friend requested you off of Facebook

"Technology, you think it's your friend but it's not."
—You've Got Mail

cOnnecTing had discOnnecTed me. Technology had become a dangerous place, the nucleus of the social media explosion in which I blew up. My online opiate den where I would wander aimlessly for hours on other people's walls, cheering them on, while I was wallowing in my own stupor of self-disgust, yet still trying to keep the digital dope pumping through my veins.

I was repulsed by the fact that I helplessly sat back as Facebook automatically shared my profile info to friends and to my friend's fun app makers like FarmVille. And of course, let's not forget all the virus advertising links I clicked on where strangers could learn where, when, how, and what I liked to inject myself with, whether it be shoes, friends, hotel sites, my password, you name it.

That is until November 16, 2012, when I logged onto my brand new iPad computer and a calendar alert popped up on my touch screen in all caps: "TWO YEAR ANNIVERSARY OF QUITTING FACE-BOOK!" Whoa, I had totally forgotten that I set the reminder on my home computer a few years ago when I was a much different person. The reminder was now synced up to my iPad and my heart.

The early stages of morphing into a former Face-booker had truly felt like an uphill battle. Those first months after I had quit Facebook were excruciatingly emotional. Severing my ties with Facebook truly was an awkward breakup. And for a while it had felt like one of the worst heartaches I had ever faced due to my involvement, I mean, my addiction to, the most powerful and handsome opiate I had ever experiment-ed with online.

I was elated to be celebrating two years of social media recovery. I had finally come to the realization that my life was easier, quieter, and more "real" now that I had finally returned to life as I once knew it, sans Facebook. My salad days of social media were over.

To celebrate, I went out on the town to wine and dine with my friend, Beth. At the bar, she looked down on her iPhone which had been buzzing nonstop with Facebook alerts for the twenty minutes since we arrived and suddenly began cackling. She interrupted our conversation and said, "Rachel, get this." She then proceeded to read aloud a post she had just received on her Facebook newsfeed from a girlfriend. "Cuddled up in a blanket by my fireplace, sipping a glass of wine."

"Beth, what is so funny about her update?" I asked.

Still laughing, she replied, "She doesn't have a fireplace."

To which I retorted, "Beth, don't laugh at the poor girl, feel sorry for her. She's a Fake-booker just like I used to be."

This woman belonged to a group of Facebook users, like my former self, that I called "Fake-bookers." I was probably a founding member of the club, a group who pretend their lives are more extravagant than they really are in order to be "friended" and "liked" more. I sadly knew the scenario Miss Non-Fireplace Facebooker was probably going through all too well. The happy-go-lucky girl I had once tried to represent myself as on Facebook was a falsehood. Facebook had once been a boasting platform for me too. I felt empathy for this woman rather than envy as I would have in the past. Two years earlier, I probably would have asked Beth to get her to friend me right that very minute in the middle of our dinner date.

I didn't enter the Shamrock race this year. Even though my foot was happily healed and securely cushioned in high-mileage running shoes, I was no longer spurred to go the extra mile solely to impress others or to gain verification that they approve of my husband's and my personal lives. I've learned to plan my activities for the sheer benefit of my own well-being and for the sincere benefit of others, such as this year's charity race event for kids with cancer where the only pictures posted of me online was done, not by me, but by a nonprofit fundraiser's website technicians.

Hallmark's "When you care enough to send the very best" jingle now rings so true. The slogan hits me on an even deeper level because when you care enough to send the best, you don't send it in the form of a posting like "Happy Birthday" or "Congratulations" or "Sorry" or a "virtual gift" on Facebook. You walk your butt to the store, you find a touching card and write something meaningful inside, you then stick a stamp on it and seal it with a lick and maybe even a kiss. To compare the Facebook inbox feeling of euphoria to discovering an envelope handwritten and addressed to you in the mailbox is impossible.

The next task on my agenda was to pick up a pen and express how much I cared for my true and sometimes neglected relationships with loved ones. I had unraveled my Facebook dependency, and successfully prevented myself from falling back onto Facebook or on to the couch to watch reality shows. I begin each new day by writing a letter or sending a box of cookies or jewelry to a different friend, whether he/she was on Facebook or not, in order to give them the true gift of correspondence. And I don't vainly look in the mailbox to check and see if they write me back.

In my opinion, a 46-cent stamp is far less costly than the time I spent on Facebook, and far more endearing than posting 200 messages a day on the walls of Facebook friends like I used to. Heck, I don't care if the price of stamps goes up tenfold; I believe the cost of sitting down to pour my heart into a handwritten letter is far more valuable than banging out a five-second Facebook post on my keyboard. In a sense, I began to imitate the art of shabby chic in interior design, where a soft and antiquated look differentiates it from modern decor, within my communication style.

I also decided to reach out to my only sibling, my sister. Once upon a time, we were best friends. But sadly, we became estranged just as I began my Facebook romance. Never once did I deem it appropriate to reach out to her on Facebook via a friend request email asking if I could add her as my friend. It seemed shallow and preposterous to connect with someone you can't connect with in person or on the phone. The last words she said to me after my elopement were "You are not my sister." Perhaps, deep down, I was afraid I would become even more crushed if she denied my Facebook request. Therefore, we never friended one another during those five years we were accessible to each other on Facebook.

Rekindling my relationship with her is still a work in progress, but going the extra effort to try to win her back as my sister and my friend, via cards and CARE packages, is now so much more meaningful than the time I spent posting messages to false friends or looking at my sister and my mutual friends' walls to try and get a glimpse of her daily life to see if she seemed happy. I would trade them all in to have my sister as my friend again.

I also started volunteering at Little Sisters of the Poor. I may not have my sister back, but I realized I could be a friend and a sister to the lonely, the elderly and to Jesus, by serving others in need with love and respect until death. Painting their nails and making Christmas decorations with the elders after closing off my Facebook wall opened so many unexpected doors, and not for me this time! For others, like the volunteer who needed help researching polycystic kidney disease because her daughter was recently diagnosed with the disease, which afflicts my family. I gave her my mother's phone number and told her to read Mom's recently published memoir, "*The Reluctant Donor.*"

Post-Facebook I found I also began attracting others in a way that I had never expected. One morning, I could almost feel a woman blanketed in sadness who had stationed her yoga mat directly behind me. Though I had no idea why I felt empathy towards her, I was compelled to reach out to her. Perhaps I did so because I knew from experience that everybody has a secret sadness inside of them like I did while on Facebook. True feelings are not completely visible on Facebook walls. And no matter how simple our friends seem on the outside or how many Facebook friends they have, inside they've all got feelings that need to be nurtured.

After class that morning, as we descended the stairs, I touched her arm and said, "Don't you love how yoga takes all of our sadness and fears and just sweats them out? This too shall pass." And then I gave her a big smile and was on my way. My words, I hoped, would bring her solace. And I sensed a glimmer of hope brimming from behind her teary eyes as I spoke to her. Or maybe I was just plain crazy.

Two days later, as I was exiting the yoga club's sliding doors, the front desk manager called me back in. "Rachel, this was left for you by someone who didn't know your name but described your features and I gave her your name" and he held out an envelope. When I got outside, I opened the envelope to discover a beautiful illustrated card and in a woman's delicate handwriting was inscribed, "Thank you for your kind words and thoughts the other day and for reaching out with compassion to someone you don't know or knew why you felt compassion towards." She went on to express how "good it was to know there are people like you in this world and in my life."

Instead of basking in her words of thanks, I fell to my knees on the concrete and cried alone in an alley behind the gym where I had locked my bicycle before class. This time I wasn't crying over a message someone posted to me, I was crying out of joy. I finally realized two years and one month after having been free of my Facebook addiction, that my Facebooking obsession had completely constipated my smooth flowing spiritual connections.

My desire to over-share my shallow status updates rather than giving out meaningful hugs had choked me. A badly-needed hug cannot equate to giving someone the "like" thumbs up button. The sad postings, which included my week-long stint of posting Eva Cassidy song lyrics about how "oh so sad" the days were, were only met with comments such as, "Don't be sad." People truly couldn't hear my desperate cries for help, nor could I hear theirs. I had suppressed my inner voice with the need to compete amidst the noise on Facebook. Only when I broke it off with Facebook did I regain sight of my own talent for communicating.

I wondered how I went from producing such a lucrative social media business, to trolling for friends. To some people, by "stripping" my Facebook account, I had soiled the social media platform I once fought for. I had finally found my voice. And it was no longer the goofy imagined one I had selfishly yearned for on Facebook.

As a Facebook user, I had failed to use my talent and my God-given gifts to create a support site for others. Instead I had dug a shallow self-esteem popularity piss pool. Here I was, a thirty- something successful journalist who had once worked for CNN and produced Emmy-award winning documentaries, but after giving up my hard-earned position in the news industry, I had lost my drive to find my true purpose in life. I was left with nothing but a burning desire to get the thumbs up button clicked on my Facebook wall. I wanted to prove my popularity to gain acceptance among my peers and bolster my sense of self-worth. In hindsight, I should have responded to those thumbs up posts of much ado about nothing with a cute baby picture photo of me with my thumb in my mouth to truly represent my online immaturity. Oh wait, I did post one. Maybe I appeared cool and even funny to some of my Facebook followers, but in my heart I was a hopeless and fanatical Facebook fool.

All that had mattered in my Facebook-frenzied mind was ensuring that no matter what I did in my free time, I would continue to build my Facebook page via a multitude of page hits and comments and new friends.

During my Facebook membership, I was filled with a superficial joy when friends populated my page with comments. Yet internally I was lonelier than ever. At the time, I firmly believed that my posts of all the fun I was having 3,000 miles away from my distant friends and family on the east coast, who were a bit shell shocked by my life choices, such as eloping with a stranger and moving cross country after only four dates, was the only means to better convince them that I was in a truly safe and happy place. Now I realize that I acted as if I were in high school all over again, as if I were dying to be cool. Ironically, I wanted to be alone with Facebook yet I was separated from the people on it. I was lonely. Now I realize the complete notion of being on Facebook to maintain friendships seems obnoxiously Helleresque, a Catch 22, to me.

My priority as a Facebook account holder was not sharing my real everyday life, but faking a fulfilling life that nevertheless always felt half-empty to me. Sometimes over-surfing and online obsessing caused me to long for someone else's Facebook fairy tale, and to forget my life story is not a collection of what was written in my status updates. Nor were some of their fairy tales actually accurate accounts of their lives that were guaranteed to come with a happy ending.

My Facebook years were just a moment in a life given especially to me by a Creator more powerful than the creators of my Facebook wall. I have no allegiance to serving Mr. Facebook. Once I stopped wasting precious time and energy on my ego, insecurities, and cyber gossip, I fully grasped the meaning of serving others using my gift of communication. I was finally strong enough to listen to the angel in me, fight my Facebook addiction and plant myself firmly on the ground rather than stumbling drunk in the quest for Mr. Facebook's love. Freedom has never tasted so good!

CHAPTER THIRTEEN

Status: Rachel Ruff has officially stepped away from the crowd

*"Friendship, without self-interest is one of
the rare and beautiful things of life."*
—*James Francis Byrnes*

i had lifTed my eyes frOm facebOOk. And as each
new day broke, so did my connection with the social
media site. I was in a relationship rebirth. One which
requires no electrical power, no Internet connection,
no passwords. By deactivating my Facebook account, I
had truly reactivated my life. While the process of deactivating my Facebook account wasn't all butterflies
and roses, happily, Ralph Waldo Emerson's quote rings
true to me now.

In the beginning, I had truly thought my romance
with Mr. Facebook would remain irrevocable. But I
finally turned social-media-celibate after I came to
admit to myself that my Facebook wall, while a good
idea in theory, just didn't quite work for me. Wise old
Emerson also once said, "Every wall is a door."

The wall I deactivated helped me open my portal to the feelings of insecurity and loneliness I had kept locked inside of me and hadn't permitted myself to explore. The five steps I created served as the gateway to exploring and processing my de-friending of Facebook. By doing so, I closed the door on my digital demons. By allowing myself to deny, grieve, and freely mourn, just as the Kubler-Ross stages of grief teaches, I was also able to close off my negative energy in order to find new avenues to reach out to others. *Step Three: I turn my will and my life over to the care of true friendships, as I understood them before Facebook.*

Facebook had been a vast abyss of self-created nightmares, where the night sky was a dark screen of LED lights. My Facebook fortress was surrounded by unsecured walls, easily scaled by hackers and frenemies. Before quitting Facebook, I could only relax at the first appearance of the rosy pink light of dawn, when an influx of inoffensive "good mornings" rolled into my Facebook news feed. Now when faced with a restless sleep, I no longer grab my iPhone to zone out into social media or to police my wall postings.

These days my mornings begin peacefully because at night I can drift away into dreams where the night sky is not a computer screen but a constellation of twinkling stars, where roses and ivy scale impenetrable stone walls, rather than the social media pals I was so frightened by on my Facebook wall. Rather than spending my days on Facebook, I am now living outside, in the real world where the beautiful blue sky isn't a glare-free screen, and the friends with whom I connect are actually tangible treasures.

At bedtime, I reach for Rebecca Rosen's book *Spirited* or Rick Warren's *The Purpose-Driven Life.* My iPhone has been evicted from its old home, the nightstand, where my favorite authors' works now permanently reside. They serve as my emotional safe haven. The words in the books gleam with their own special guidance.

In *Spirited*, Rosen helps readers learn how to tune into the "spirit energy" of our loved ones who have passed. She explains that your inner self has to be very quiet to hear these "spirit voices," such as during a peaceful walk on a beach. I wonder how she would address being in places such as Facebook and other social networking sites. Might they affect, perhaps even thwart or even crowd out, our ability to hear spirit voices?

Rosen writes, "Let go of any negative energy so you can replace it with positive energy. When we're full of positive energy, we have less room for the nasty stuff to come creeping back in. Makes sense, right?"

My answer to that question was a loud, "Hell, yeah!"

Facebook was standing in my way because I was not using the site like some good citizens do to help build villages in third world countries or to help raise money for medical research to find cures to diseases. By creating the Facebook Anonymous steps, I was able to rebuild my soul and shift my heart in a different direction towards serving others rather than using others opinions about me and my life on Facebook to serve my egotistical insecurities. *The Purpose-Driven Life* taught me not to trade my life for temporary things. Warren asks, "What are you allowing to stand in the way of your mission?"

Just one month shy of quitting Facebook, I had been diagnosed with Obsessive Compulsive Disorder, which I felt embarrassed about because a lot of nasty stuff interrupted my daily thoughts. My OCD diagnosis was discovered, not because of my Facebook addiction, but because of repetitive OCD thoughts that I was exhibiting such as "did I lock the door?" or "did I turn the oven off?" and sometimes from even more disturbing thought obsessions like "Did I cause the wildfires in Boulder?" even though I lived in a city 30 miles away. However, I was proud and not embarrassed by the fact that quitting Facebook did help quiet my OCD fears immensely because the noise level in my head from worrying about other people's posts suddenly went silent.

In one in-depth OCD therapy session, my therapist taught me to distract my "looping worries" with a peaceful activity such as singing, which I definitely can't do, or painting, which I can, to calm the amygdala, the "fight or flight" center of the brain, where OCD is triggered.

My OCD was quieted and my spirit voice came through in the form of my paintings when I finally picked up my paintbrush instead of picking through others' status updates. When I embarked on the first painting I had done in over two years, dipping my brush into the oils felt liberating. Back in DC, I had quit coming home from a stressful day at work to dive into my art supplies when I got enmeshed in Facebook.

During tough times in life, I have used art to help heal whatever hardships I was facing. And my paintings truly reflect what I am going through. If there is a lot of black on the canvas, I was feeling sadness. Or if I was just given a job promotion, there would be a frenzy of flowers splayed across the board. This first post-Facebook painting revealed to me that I had been dealing with a lot of buzzing in my ears. Before me stood a 24 X 24-inch painting depicting an intricate honeycomb crawling with honey bees.

Bees are beautiful creatures. Yet I am scared of them if I come across a large nest filled with the sounds of a lot of angry buzzing. I step away. Now I feel the same about my friends while on Facebook. They are all beautiful individuals, but mesh them into one Facebook list or one buzzing hive and I became vulnerable to painful stings.

My nights are also much more peaceful because I no longer stay awake tossing and turning in worry that during my slumber someone might sting me by posting a troublesome message to my Facebook wall. These days, instead of grabbing my laptop to monitor the latest Facebook postings I missed while sleeping, I wake with a refreshed mind and spirit no longer plagued with looping worries of posts I cannot control. I love spending my time looking at the pretty flowers while pulling out the weeds in my garden, rather than sowing hatred and discontent on Facebook and deleting the weeds others had planted on my wall for me to water with my tears.

When I was struggling to get over my addiction, I used to repeatedly hum Johnny Cash's powerful song, "Ring of Fire" that he wrote about his demons of substance addiction. I am no longer in the ring of Facebook fire nor am I concerned with what others are posting on Facebook or think of me in real life. Not even one drop of Facebook anxiety pours from the sweat of my brow onto my yoga mat anymore. For once and for all, I am listening to my own spirit. Truly, finally, beautifully. No thumbs up needed.

I'm no social media savant, though. I still get sick and tired of the "You're not on Facebook?!" responses when people I meet ask me to friend them. I tell them I quit Facebook and I often get the same shotgun response, "Oh, I'm on Facebook…but I don't really use it." I joked to one of my friends who fired that response back to me, "You can admit to using porn sites to me but you are too embarrassed to confess you surf Facebook!?" To which he replied, "Well, I don't have your pictures available on my Facebook wall anymore to service my sexual needs." Gross. I almost threw up.

I had naively assumed that by "putting out" my Facebook messages by the minute and proudly tagging myself in pictures, that I could enhance my relationships and increase my day-to-day interactions with friends. But I got nothing in return from my digital displays but anxiety and grief.

Those four, formless years I had spent being active with Mr. Facebook are a complete fallacy to me now.

I was in a state of digital delusion. My sexy holiday-themed costumes, like those Lady Gaga fishnets, the spread-eagle poses of myself mounted on a chopper bike in Daisy Duke short shorts, and my delectable desserts were all done in vain. To use a Carrie quote from "Sex & The City," "I revealed too much too soon. I was socially slutty."

By following my five-step program, I was able to admit to myself that I needed to step off the social media platform I was repeatedly diving into headfirst and crashing. Vanity had taken precedence over my sanity. I simply could not find a happy medium even though I tried to trick myself into believing I could just slow down with Mr. Facebook, "If I don't really share anything with him like my thoughts or photos and just use him to look at my friends' baby pictures, I'll be okay," was what the devil tried to brainwash me into believing. Thankfully, I listened to my angel, my inner voice, and during the dinner party from digital hell I finally snapped and broke up with him.

Karl used to say to me, "You know you and your friends are in a cult. I swear, Facebook is a cult." And he was right. Like Living Colour's song goes, I was in a "cult of personality." And I wasn't singing any praises for the effort I had put into trying to impress the cult.

A girlfriend recently confided to me, "Rachel, I decided to give it [quitting] a try too. I am so shocked at how relieved I am for doing it. People don't realize how freeing it feels to finally get the monkey [Facebook] off your back. Everybody is so scared to say anything negative about Facebook. In fact everyone is so hesitant that they don't even quit their Facebook, they simply say, 'Oh well, I don't really post anything on Facebook, I—'

"...I just use it to look at my friends' baby pictures!" I interjected.

She squeezed my hand hard and tossed her head back laughing. "Exactly! Don't they realize that they are underwriting the IPO even if they don't 'use' their Facebook account?"

"Nope, but you know what? That doesn't bother me anymore. The price we paid on Facebook is all moot now, we're free!"

This year I had a lovely and quiet birthday. I received ten happy birthday phone calls and six birthday cards and two presents. A smaller number, but much more valuable than the virtual gifts or 200 messages I had received from Facebook friends in the past. While I had purged over a thousand loose Facebook friends by deactivating my account, I gave myself the gift of realizing who my real friends are, and in doing so I became a better friend to myself, too.

A few of my Facebook friends went on to become some of my "real" friends. Nikki, a true buddy during and subsequent to my Facebook usage, recently said to me on a girl's night out, "You know what, Rach, I'm glad you're off Facebook now. I used to be lazy and just post to your wall. Now I go, 'damn, she's not on Facebook anymore. Guess I'll have to call her up tomorrow and do yoga or coffee to catch up.' I like that."

And I do too.

As of today, I am officially three years, and I don't know how many days, or how many hours, Facebook sober. I've stopped counting. My name is Rachel, which in Hebrew, means "little lamb." I am not a black sheep even though my status is "non-Facebook user." I just needed to move on to greener and quieter pastures.

I wandered lonely as a cloud
That floats on high o'er vales and hills,
When all at once I saw a crowd,
A host, of golden daffodils;
—William Wordsworth

The End.

ABOUT THE AUTHOR

Rachel Ruff is an award-winning CNN producer turned ad-agency executive. Ruff served as the Vice President of Porter Novelli in Washington, DC, where she used her media industry insight and extensive CNN experience to oversee digital media and broadcast media projects.

Rachel Ruff managed and produced the "Dr. Sanjay Gupta Primetime" documentaries at CNN and created segments related to food and health for the CNN "American Morning" show. She earned the honor of being the youngest producer for the network in 1997 and produced the first-ever "World Aids Day" documentary in 2004.

Rachel graduated from the University of Florida with a communications degree and a pre-med concentration and holds a Pastry Arts degree with Honors from L'Academie De Cuisine in Gaithersburg, Maryland. She completed an externship working for White House chefs Anne Amernick and Frank Ruta.

In the spring of 2013, her original salmon recipe was published by Penguin in the Pike Place Fish Guys cookbook, the dish earned placement as a cover photo.

Rachel resides in Denver, Colorado and is working on her next book.

Made in the USA
Columbia, SC
01 October 2021